IN NATURE'S SLIPSTREAM

This book is dedicated to the reader.
I hope it is the start of a wonderful adventure.

IN NATURE'S SLIPSTREAM

How to turn your garden into a haven for nature

CAROL BRUCE

CONTENTS

INTRODUCTION *6*

Chapter One ABOUT THE GARDEN *14*

Chapter Two A TOUR OF THE GARDEN *26*

Chapter Three GOING FERAL *76*

Chapter Four GROWING PERENNIAL
                SPECIES FROM SEED *94*

Chapter Five DESIGN OBSERVATIONS *136*

Chapter Six DESIGN TECHNIQUES *152*

Chapter Seven STAYING IN CONTROL *188*

Chapter Eight APPROACHING A BLANK CANVAS *202*

CONCLUSION *210*

INDEX *217*

ACKNOWLEDGMENTS *222*

ABOUT THE AUTHOR *224*

INTRODUCTION

Left: The wooded valleys are a constantly changing landscape of light and life.

Bladbean is a tiny hamlet surrounded by woods high up on the west side of the beautiful Elham Valley in Kent, so I am blessed with wonderful countryside to walk in every morning right on my doorstep. By walking in them daily over the years, the woods and lanes have become my home territory on a very instinctive level. I have observed every tiny detail of the wild plant communities, the variety of habitats, the birds and animals that live here, the lie of the land, and the circle of life through the seasons. Walking alone has allowed the information and emotion to reach the most creative part of my mind, and I carry these experiences back into my little world behind the wall and stitch them into the tapestry of ideas, feelings, and actions that become the garden.

The drive to create a garden as an outer expression of my bond with nature has been with me since childhood.

Through this solitary and observant relationship with the surrounding countryside, a touch of elemental wonder and enchantment has worked its way into the garden which is palpable to everyone who comes here. This is no accident – it is the result of the methodical study of my own emotional responses to particular views or aspects of the countryside. I isolated and extracted the key elements and then recreated them deliberately within my garden's design, so a distillation of everything that moves me on a fundamental level in the woods and lanes is quite literally woven into the fabric of my garden.

The drive to create a garden as an outer expression of my bond with nature has been with me since childhood. It became the motivation for making my way in life, from training as an economist to getting a job, buying a house, and eventually moving to this magical place hidden in the woods where the influence and energy of nature are so strong that they define every aspect of daily life. In 2003 aged 33, I was finally ready to start work on the ground, and being able to work in peace and quiet meant that I could dissolve the boundary between my inner and outer worlds and create a place that is a fusion of both.

My relationship with the garden is so complex that it is very hard to decide where gardening stops and the garden starts. The two combine in an intricate dynamic, and while the place is distinct from the activity of tending it the garden itself is really more of a consequence than anything else, rather like a singer and their song. For me this makes both the garden and the act of continually creating it endlessly rewarding – cause and consequence are engaged in a dance that never ends, and one validates and justifies the other.

> In many ways gardens trigger instincts that we are all born with, but that modern life gives us very few ways to experience or express.

In many ways gardens trigger instincts that we are all born with, but that modern life gives us very few ways to experience or express. While these instincts are geared towards an ancestral way of life in a wild and potentially dangerous environment, we can relax in the knowledge that there are no bears and wolves in our little plots. Our gardens are uniquely contemplative spaces because we can tap into ancient and unexpressed elements of ourselves without the need to be alert for danger: in gardens we have invented our own little Edens where we can feel both safe and free.

Creating the garden here was part of a much broader reassessment of my relationship with the natural world, as in 2000 I thought through the likely course and consequences of climate change and realized we needed to radically alter the way we live. Modern democratic societies appeared to be incompatible with the degree and speed of change that would be required. People are far too individualistic, entitled, and empowered to accept the necessary degree of constraint, and social hierarchies are tied to resource ownership and display, so materialism is wired into the social psyche. Pushing from the front just wasn't going to work. I needed to design a new way of living within nature's constraints, a way of relating to the natural world that was not about dominance, control, exploitation, and ownership, but was rather about accepting nature's dominance and developing techniques, values, and attitudes that respectfully harness natural systems instead of damaging them. I have been working out an integrated system of values, goals, and behaviours that will conform not to social expectations but to the need to live a meaningful and rewarding life without harming Mother Nature. It is not a new approach to living of course, as by working

> In gardens we have invented our own little Edens where we can feel both safe and free.

from first principles and using deductive problem-solving methods, I have ended up as something akin to a Stoic, but it is certainly a new, independently derived, and authentic way of being for me.

Restricting my exposure to culture, fashion, and other social influences was key to this process because the inner voice is so easily drowned out by the noise of the crowd, and inner vision is quickly obscured by the wall of images that come our way in human environments. Hidden away in the woods free from the influence of existing schools of thought, I was able to engage with the raw power of natural systems and that same wild inheritance within myself, and bring the two together to create a garden and a way of life that is as close to the wild as it can possibly be without losing control.

> It is said that a garden is a reflection of your soul and that is certainly true for me.

While I was always driven to create a garden, there was an added source of urgency. At the age of 28 I was diagnosed and treated for thyroid cancer, a disease with a very long follow-up period as it can recur at any time over the next 20 years. I had to come to terms with my mortality at the most driven and energetic age in life, and knowing that whatever I committed to or dared to care about might have to survive without me severely limited my options. It felt like I had lost security of tenure over my own body and had to learn a new way of living with a gun to my head. Unlike most people at that age who vaguely presume the second half of life will be the time for such projects, I felt the urgency to get the garden out of my mind and onto the ground as quickly as I could to ensure it would see the light of day. I also needed something that I could love and nurture but that wouldn't miss me if I died, and a garden was the perfect candidate. In a very physical way, the garden became the container for my life force, passion, and sense of future that no longer had a safe home within me. I have been really moved that visitors can feel the intensity of this love and the very feminine and nurturing relationship I have with my garden, as it never occurred to me that it would leave such a palpable trace.

It is said that a garden is a reflection of your soul and that is certainly true for me. Indeed, it is a replica of my inner sanctuary, but by complete accident it also works to communicate my inner world to other people in a language that they can instantly understand. Like me or loathe me, no-one misunderstands me any more. In creating the garden, I have made my inner world manifest, and I welcome people to wander around it in the knowledge that what they are experiencing tells my truth. At long last no-one presumes to tell me who I am and in itself that is liberating and validating, but it has also shown me just how many thoughtful, self-aware, and broadminded people there are in the world who are genuinely happy to share my passion with curiosity and respect.

I was born at home, and at a couple of hours old I was sleeping peacefully in a basket under a leafy tree, and I am sure this set the tone for my entire life. I have a direct emotional connection to nature and as a result I never feel lonely, separated, or lost but rather supported, loved, and at peace. Gardening for me feels like tending this relationship with love and care in the same way that people look after each other. The longer I garden and the more I experiment, the more I am convinced that natural systems and gardening are compatible, and that our gardens can be a sanctuary and a celebration of the natural world without losing the features that make them so loved and familiar to us all.

Building the walls and paths for my garden generated a lot of coming and going along the narrow country lanes and all this activity attracted attention. With an increasing number of local people asking to see it, in 2012 I decided to open the garden to visitors through the National Garden Scheme (NGS) to let everyone who was interested come and have a look around. Rather than quelling curiosity, word started to spread, and so I continue to open the garden every summer simply to share the beauty and joy it brings with anyone who wants to visit.

> The longer I garden and the more I experiment, the more I am convinced that natural systems and gardening are compatible.

Opening a garden through the NGS requires you to fix the dates a year in advance, and while I had a vague notion of what flowered when, I realized the value of having a more precise way to decide which dates to pick. With the garden so far off the beaten track, I was also keen to provide prospective visitors with as much information as possible about what would be in bloom on the available dates, so in 2015 I started taking a set of photographs every day between 1st May and 31st August to use as a record of flowering times and to post on my garden website. I soon found getting up just after dawn and wandering around the garden with a camera so absorbing and enjoyable that it became the highpoint of my day. I developed an interest in why certain photographs were more effective than others, to the point where I enjoyed the art of taking them as much as the experience of being a visitor in my own garden at such a peaceful time of day.

To make the daily summer photographs more widely available to garden visitors, I started a Facebook page in 2016 and began daily posts with written descriptions, which

INTRODUCTION

became highly enjoyable in itself. The posts attracted visitors to the garden from far and wide, many of whom had not even heard of the NGS. To keep Facebook followers up to date with the garden out of season, I also began taking photographs weekly through the rest of the year, and as a result I now have a comprehensive record of the garden and its plants comprising thousands of images.

> I now have a comprehensive record of the garden and its plants comprising thousands of images.

In 2022 I was grateful to be given a chance to explain my approach to gardening and to share my work here with a wider audience through BBC *Gardeners' World*, and in 2023 the garden was voted winner of the Nation's Favourite Gardens competition for the South East by readers of *The English Garden* magazine. The experience of sharing my work with the wider world has been illuminating and fascinating. So rarely in the past have my motives and methods been understood that I gave up trying to share them and wandered off into the woods. To stand before the world and share my truth and for it to be understood has been a fortifying experience, and I am very grateful for the encouragement that it has brought.

So many gardeners got in touch as a result of the feature on *Gardeners' World*, and I was struck by how similar their questions were to those asked by visitors on NGS open days. They wanted to know how I designed the garden by myself with no training, how I maintain it entirely on my own, and how I imbued it with such a distinctive, otherworldly feel. They wanted to know how I embrace natural selection to keep the garden vibrant and healthy without irrigation, pesticides, or fertilizer, how I prolong the flowering season without deadheading, and how it functions as an ornamental ecosystem to provide food and shelter for wildlife. Above all, they wanted to know how to do these things at home.

> I will show you how to transform your plot into an ornamental ecosystem that thrives entirely within the constraints of nature.

I have written this book in response to their questions to share my methods and observations in the hope that other gardeners can benefit from my experiences here. In the chapters ahead we will take a tour of the garden together, stopping to investigate the old roses along the way, and then explore the surrounding countryside to discover how to forge a new balance between wild and cultivated environments without jeopardising the look of a well-tended garden. I will show you how to transform your plot into an ornamental ecosystem that thrives entirely within the constraints of nature, including the plants I use to ensure its health and beauty, and I will share the design techniques I developed to create my garden so that you can use them in your own. We will explore the methods and mindset needed to tackle a blank canvas and to maintain three acres of garden alone, and I will leave you with some project ideas to try at home.

While most gardeners have been trying to add back natural elements to traditionally cultivated gardens, I have been working in from the wild side. I hope to meet you as you explore more nature-friendly methods of gardening, and to hand you something that can be integrated into a garden environment in the knowledge that it has been tried and tested here for over 20 years.

Right: With the right techniques, a garden doesn't have to look wild to live by nature's rules.

When I started the garden here in 2003, the site was a blank canvas and I had very little gardening knowledge or experience. This gave me the rare opportunity to design the garden and figure out the maintenance methods within the boundaries of my own gardening philosophy so that they could all work together as a holistic system. In this chapter I outline my gardening philosophy and explain its impact on the garden's design, maintenance methods, and plant choices. I also share an overview of my design process, and a brief history of the garden together with my thoughts on its future.

Chapter One

ABOUT THE GARDEN

Left: Flowering perennial species self-sow across the rose garden paths.

ABOUT THE GARDEN

A HOLISTIC SYSTEM

Right: Allium hollandicum
and a humble snail are equally
treasured here as part of the
circle of life.

Establishing a gardening philosophy had to come first, as it would set the parameters for what was going to be possible and acceptable in terms of maintenance and plant choices. I thought through the principles I wanted to impose on the project to make sure it would be entirely aligned with my values, and the resulting philosophy can be summarized as follows.

To respect nature above all things and in all things: I am in awe of Mother Nature, have complete respect for natural systems and processes, and I would no more set myself against them than presume to hold back the sea. Everything I do in the garden, indeed in life, is approached as an act of reverence for nature, and while I deliberately and gratefully harness the power of natural systems to achieve my goals, I would never defy them.

> Everything I do in the garden, indeed in life, is approached as an act of reverence for nature.

To set and work within binding constraints: not only do I acknowledge and work under the constraints of natural systems, but I also set and work within binding constraints myself. The relentless stream of ideas that accompanies me through life is of no use to anyone if I can't marshal it into some sort of order, and to do this I have always imposed constraints on myself to act as guide rails within which my ideas can coalesce into something I can act on. So much in life is like doing a jigsaw puzzle where you need to start with the edges, so I seek out edges and when I can't find any, I create them.

To innovate rather than imitate: self-reliance is fundamental to my nature, and when faced with a problem to solve it doesn't even occur to me to look to other people as I'm just not wired up to copy. I am, however, observant, inventive, and methodical, so my default way to make decisions is to work things out from first principles then use trial and error to settle on a solution. The implications of this are

profound: I am motivated to produce and develop original ideas completely to the exclusion of imitating or adopting what other people have done. This is why I deliberately avoided any form of training before I started the project, and it is why I come up with novel, if sometimes eccentric, ways of doing things.

In essence my gardening philosophy, indeed my personal philosophy, is committed to the innovation of original ideas independent of cultural influence within the binding constraints of nature and the guide rails of self-imposed discipline. How does this influence the choices I made in the design and contents of the garden and how I look after it?

My gardening philosophy placed clear constraints on how I could manage the garden: to work within the natural conditions of the site there could be no watering, no chemical treatment of pests and diseases, no fertilizers, no organic matter added or taken away, and no protection from the elements. The garden would have to fit in and adapt to its environment or it could not exist at all. Self-imposed constraints further determined how I would approach the project, and I committed to spending five hours a day mastering everything myself, from the design and gardening methods, to the day-to-day maintenance work.

The impact of this on the garden's plants and design was profound. I needed to create a garden that stood the best chance of thriving under these terms, which meant choosing plants that were already adapted to my conditions and allowing them to live out their days as close as possible to how they would grow in the wild. As my garden would be exposed to the same selection pressure as the surrounding countryside, I came up with the idea of creating an ornamental ecosystem with self-sowing populations of flowering hardy perennial species instead of individual named varieties. This would harness natural selection through survival of the fittest – nature's tried and tested mechanism for steering the biosphere into alignment with the sky above and the earth below. It also determined what I could grow here: genetically diverse perennial species from similar climates around the world, native and local wildflowers and roses proven for hundreds of years to survive unaided, but no pots, tender perennials, bedding plants, or half-hardy annuals that would need watering during the growing season.

The garden's design was influenced by my philosophy in other ways beyond its impact on the choice of plants. The twin themes of self-imposed discipline and reverence for nature are visible everywhere: in the relationship between the layouts and the planting, in the tension between the strict colour schemes and the profusion of flowers, and in the feral energy of the self-sowing plant communities punctuated by the stern figures of box and yew.

The garden started life destined to be an integrated system and it has grown more tight-knit over the years via feedback from its maintenance and the climate. Species that thrive under the regime have increased in number while others have dwindled, and I am endlessly tweaking my methods to see what the effect will be on the garden as an ecosystem, particularly regarding the timing of different jobs through the year. Innovation, respect for nature, self-reliance, and discipline define this place, and its character and vitality are the result of an approach that always respects constraints, puts the needs of the system ahead of the individual, and responds with reverence rather than defiance to nature's ways.

MY DESIGN PROCESS

A common question among visitors is how I conjured up the garden designs with no training, so before we take a tour through the five different garden areas, here is an explanation of my design process.

I started by deciding on the emotions I wanted the finished area to evoke, and identifying features of the space I couldn't change such as the amount of visible sky, large trees, boundaries, and buildings. Then I built these into imaginary places in my mind's eye and wandered around them to see what emotions I experienced, how many lines of sight the layouts generated, and what the journey around the garden and through the seasons would look and feel like. I changed things around in my head until it generated the desired feelings, and it was rather like building and then visiting my own private Narnia.

Anything that provoked the target emotions got included at this stage, be it music, poetry, paintings, films, animals, plants, places, people, myths and fairytales, legends and belief systems, landscapes, or just my own memories. They were all thrown into the mix and woven into the thousands of tiny choices that went together to generate the finished place. Once I had something that worked emotionally, I fixed the entire image as a visual memory of a place I hadn't actually been to yet. At this stage the image was composed of the colours, textures, shapes, and sizes of the plants but with no specific plants in mind, so my imagination was not constrained by the limits of my existing knowledge. This part of the process went on in the back of my mind while I was walking in the countryside, and for several months it became the primary focus of my inner world.

Right: Everyday scenes can be a masterclass in composition: this country lane demonstrates the power of perspective, proportion, focal point, and framing.

Next came the factual, methodical, and detailed part which involved analysing the image from all aspects and working backwards to decide on the components needed to create a replica on the ground. This took up to four months of research and planning, and by the end of this process I had made a scale layout and planting plan of the new garden area. Once the scale plans were complete, it was then too late to make small changes as all the elements of the design were interwoven and interdependent.

The final part of the process was actually building the garden, which required lots of scheduling, organising, lugging, digging, and determination to turn plans on paper into a scaled-up living reality on the ground. At this stage I also needed to work out the quantity of plants and then how to source or grow them. The planting part of the process involved me pacing about with a clipboard talking to myself, waving garden canes and string about, and meticulously positioning what often looked like dead sticks all over what looked like a field of mud. This was rather unfortunate as it was also the first time the design took a form that made it visible to anyone else!

Throughout the process I deliberately isolated myself from sources of knowledge on garden design and avoided visiting other gardens in order to keep my creative palette pristine. I think entirely visually and have always been able to conjure up entire places in my mind's eye, but at the same time being highly visual I am strongly impacted by everything that I see. I wanted to make sure that my mental drawing board had a chance to fill with images welling up from within rather than to create a garden that was derived from external secondary sources, so I decided it was best to work in complete isolation.

Instead, the surrounding countryside was the primary source of ideas for the designs, just as it was for my gardening philosophy, the garden's maintenance methods, and even some of the wildflower strains that grow here. I studied the woodlands, lanes, and open countryside to learn how I responded to different natural landscapes, and then applied this knowledge to the garden. Tight transitions between different areas, an emphasis on lines of sight, immersive planting,

intermingled perennial colonies, successional planting within fixed roles, creating a sense of journey, three storeys of planting, restricted colour schemes, narrow and curved trails, symmetrical repeating verticals, and the hypnotic power of perspective – all these design features came directly from my experiences while out walking. Responses to such features are very elemental and universal, and they give the garden an enchanted otherworldly feel quite unlike anywhere else.

For me gardening is a very artistic activity, so I regard the space as a blank canvas, conceive of the design as a landscape composition, and then work backwards to select suitable components from the material world to render the image as a living collage on the ground. Only when I am happy with the composition conceived in its entirety in my mind do I start considering which components to use. This process leaves its mark on the appearance of the garden in several ways. It throws emphasis onto big picture elements such as layout, lines of sight, routes, landmarks, transitions, and colour schemes, and it naturally produces a very unified garden "livery" of structural planting and hard landscaping materials.

Initiating the design process with colour, texture, size, and form but not with specific plants influences my eventual plant choices, as they are selected to fulfil preordained roles within the view. I audition plant options for the specific roles, so considerations such as fashion, familiarity, or availability do not affect my choices as they otherwise could. Working this way also has an influence on the area I give over to a specific plant, as it is determined by what looks right within the whole imaginary composition rather than by convention or habit, and so larger scale views are often matched by larger patch sizes than would otherwise be the case.

> The act of materialising something from my imagination onto the ground is very much akin to making a copy.

Before I started work on the garden here, I had little experience or knowledge beyond the usual childhood memories of sowing seeds and helping out in our small family garden, so I turned to the internet to search for suitable herbaceous hardy perennials and I chose the rose varieties with the aid of sellers' online catalogues. I honestly don't think my garden would be here without the internet, as it gave me access to almost limitless plant information at the touch of a button without jeopardizing my solitary approach to the whole project.

The act of materialising something from my imagination onto the ground is very much akin to making a copy, with the original still lodged inside my head. This makes the process less daunting, as it is just a case of choosing components and sequencing the elements of the project to get it done within the constraints of space and time. Without fully formed imaginary gardens serving as both motivation and blueprint I would not have been able to do any of this. I am in debt to my neurodiverse wiring for giving me hyperphantasia, synaesthesia, hyperfocus, sensory hypersensitivity, visual hyper-systemizing cognition, and hyper-attention to detail, as they all played distinct and vital roles in the process. In the design observations and design techniques chapters ahead, I share some of what I learned while designing the garden in a way that will be accessible to everyone.

THE HISTORY AND FUTURE OF THE GARDEN
I moved to Old Bladbean Stud in 2003 with my husband who was looking for a country house to renovate, and it came with an acre of scruffy lawn and two acres of abandoned ground covered with nettles, thistles, old huts, and broken concrete. While I was always driven to create a garden from scratch, it had to be on a vacant site as I understand how much love goes into a garden, and to rip up an existing one would feel like vandalism. Here I found the perfect blank canvas where I could work without feeling conflicted. Everything about the situation was right: I was between jobs so I had time on my hands, the site was hidden from the road so I could work in privacy, and I was in good health and very grateful to life for throwing me this opportunity. Morning dog walks in the surrounding countryside were a fertile creative trigger and soon my imagination was full of ideas jostling to be let out onto the ground.

Given its size I decided to divide most of the plot into a sequence of five separate areas and connect them with a route, and then I deliberately started work on the area destined to be the rose garden because it was furthest from the house. This was to give me the incentive to complete the rest of the project and not leave it stranded on the far side of a scruffy field looking rather like an abandoned holiday resort. I drew up the layout and hard landscaping plan, and a local contractor built the wall and the rose garden paths in the summer of 2003 while I spent three months working on the planting plan.

With occasional help from my husband, the soil was prepared and the bare-root plants, shrubs, and trees were planted during the winter of 2003/2004. The following summer I grew the seed-raised herbaceous perennials and worked out the rose garden's maintenance needs to gauge how much time this would leave me to care for the rest of the garden that was to follow. I worked my way across the site adding

ABOUT THE GARDEN

one new garden area at a time in a similar manner, and construction for the final piece of the puzzle was completed in 2009, with the planting finished in 2011. Once the garden was fully laid out, I concentrated my gardening time entirely on maintaining it, and in the years that followed I experimented with the methods and timings of the different jobs to settle on a routine that fits with the yearly cycles of the plants and the weather.

> It was always my intention that the fate of the garden should mirror my own.

It was always my intention that the fate of the garden should mirror my own, and at over 20 years old now, it is fully mature. While I haven't noticed the effects of age yet, it is only natural that in the years ahead I will start to slow down, and because its future is entirely tied to mine, as I lose strength so will the garden. This land belonged to Mother Nature before I started to manipulate it, and when the time comes I am very happy for her to reclaim it with her wild and enchanting ways. I will always be grateful that she gave me the time to put my emotional landscapes on the ground at all.

Left: Despite the illusion of permanence, the garden was created to be cherished in the moment.

When visitors arrive at the garden, they walk up a scruffy gravel drive and past an old ugly barn, with no indication of what lies hidden behind the wall. This makes an important point: my garden is a secret, private place completely invisible from the road, and only those who actively seek it out realize there is anything here to see at all. So let us start our tour of the garden by walking up the scruffy drive, pushing open the wrought iron gate in the rose garden wall, and stepping into another world.

Chapter Two

A TOUR OF THE GARDEN

Left: Just inches away from the gravel drive, geraniums, alliums, delphiniums, and roses merge into a fairytale landscape of flowers.

THE ROSE GARDEN

Left: The visitor becomes part of the picture as they wander along the narrow paths obscured by a profusion of flowers.

As a child I was entranced by the photographic images of old English rose gardens on jigsaw puzzles and birthday cards, but I grew up to realize the sense of profusion and immersion was just the result of clever camera angles. In making my rose garden, I set out to rewrite the end of the story by turning those illusions into a real place on the ground that can be walked through and viewed from every angle without turning out to be trick of the lens.

I also wanted stepping into the rose garden to feel like stumbling across an enchanted glade, so I used as many features as I could from the surrounding woodlands to capture this effect. There is a strong imprint of narrow forest trails in the layout, and I tried to recreate the chance alignments and glimpses across and through the plants that I find so enchanting in the woods.

> A place so dense with flowers you can almost believe fairies are hiding around every corner.

I deliberately obscured views out of the rose garden leaving the trails as the main lines of sight, and the maze-like layout ensures unexpected views lie hidden around every corner. A key feature of the local woodlands is the way plant communities work in storeys: there is an upper canopy of tall trees, a middle storey of smaller trees and large shrubs, and an understorey of flowering perennials and groundcover plants. I decided to mimic this in the rose garden to capture the feel of being in woodland on an instinctive level. These elements all work together to give a "lost in the woods" charm to the rose garden, which is an important part of its identity, and by incorporating them into a place so dense with flowers you can almost believe there are fairies hiding around every corner.

The rose garden was laid out in a fan shape on an area of ground 120 feet long by 90 feet wide, with three concentric curved paths crossing four long straight ones that radiate from a single point. The paths divide the space into ten separate beds in a range of shapes and sizes and create four long straight views to an angel sculpture (Pete Moorhouse, *Angel*, 2004, 1.25m edition), while the curved paths reveal a succession of views as you walk along their length. I was keen to explore the role of lines of sight on the experience of moving through a space and capture the complex dynamic between the observer and the observed, so with the exception of the wall bed there is no front or back to any of the beds. This means that as you move, they fall into an endless range of alignments depending on your point of view. The angel sculpture is the counterpoint to this, as she simultaneously observes in every direction while acting as a fixed landmark on the journey around the maze of paths.

The site of the rose garden was already surrounded by native deciduous trees, and this generates a distinctive, dappled woodland light that is enchanting at sunrise and in the early evening. There are more than 80 different varieties of rose growing here, and the beds are dotted with flowering shrubs such as *Kolkwitzia amabilis*, *Syringa*, *Hibiscus*, *Weigela*, *Amelanchier lamarckii*, *Viburnum* and *Buddleja alternifolia* to bolster the larger roses and create an effective and varied middle storey. The ground is completely covered with a dense self-sowing understorey of flowering perennial species that keeps the soil moist and cool and provides food and shelter for wildlife. Growing conditions vary widely in the rose garden, from full shade with permanently damp soil behind the angel sculpture, to bone dry with full sun in front of the large trees on the north boundary with the neighbouring field. Just under the topsoil some beds are chalky rubble, some flaky red gravel, and others have giant flints embedded in sticky orange clay, but the self-sowing understorey takes the varied conditions in its stride.

The majority of the roses are very old once-flowering varieties, and although their flowering time is highly dependent on the weather, they are usually in bloom between early June and early July. A quarter of the roses do repeat flower in August, but the rose garden is a place of extremes by its very nature, as after their first flush old roses produce an untidy jungle of new stems, and these are trained into position over the winter to produce the best flowers the following year.

PLANTING, PRUNING, AND TRAINING THE ROSES
All the roses here were planted between November 2003 and February 2004 as dormant bare-rooted plants with a handful of bonemeal, and they took very well, producing vigorous new growth in their first season. A few were subsequently moved

but their growth was permanently set back as a result, so it is probably best to view the initial planting position as permanent. A couple of pot-grown roses were also planted during the growing season but they never lived up to their bare-rooted equivalents. In the first year, growth was all about establishing a framework of branches to bear flowers the following summer, and the plants matured to a steady state three or four years after planting.

With so many aspects of gardening you only get out what you put in, and this is spectacularly true with roses. I spend the entire of December pruning and training roses and every year I carry out renewal pruning, which involves removing all the oldest stems at the base, shortening side shoots to two buds on remaining mature wood, and removing the spindly tips of the new main stems that grew in the summer just passed. The roses here receive no water, fertilizer, or protection from pests and diseases, so their performance is entirely due to the way they are pruned and trained. On the rare occasion that I have accidentally missed pruning one, the impact has been drastic. They have been pruned in this way since their third year in the ground, and apart from six lost to silverleaf, they are all still vigorous and healthy 21 years later.

> With so many aspects of gardening you only get out what you put in, and this is spectacularly true with roses.

One of the reasons the old shrub roses fell out of favour with modern gardeners is their rather chaotic habit in the second half of the summer, when new growth can flail right across paths and flowerbeds. These long pliable stems looked ideal for tying to supports, so I decided to plant them in groups of three and train the stems over metal domes to produce what look like enormous and very well-behaved rose bushes. Training them in this way means I can keep almost all of the new growth, rather than having to shorten the main stems to stop them from falling over under the weight of flowers. The domes provide structure and support during the flowering season, hold the flowers clear of the perennial carpet below, and allow new growth to go straight up through the metal bars once flowering is over.

In their quest to attract pollinators, roses always aim to flower as high up as possible, so a stem growing upright will naturally flower at the very end. When the end is cut off and the stem trained into a more horizontal position the plant isn't sure which bud is highest, so it breaks into bloom all along the stem and produces up to ten clusters of flowers instead of just one or two. Training roses over the domes is the most time-consuming job in the whole garden as every year all the stems are untied, the old ones are pruned out, and then the remaining stems are arched into horizontal positions and tied back onto the domes. The whole process takes about three hours per dome, and it is a wonderfully forward-looking way to spend the darkest days of winter.

The roses are something of an outlier here, as unlike most of the other flowering plants, they are all named varieties – genetic clones propagated by grafting. As such I think of them as genetic works of art rather than links in the chain of the garden's gene pool, and there is less to gain from letting them set seed, so throughout the main rose season I wander daily through the rose garden, snapping off spent flowers with a joyful grin on my face. Old rose varieties usually bear their flowers in clusters of five to ten buds that open sequentially, and removing faded flowers not only keeps them looking their best but also deters the bush from shedding the last few buds unopened. With few exceptions the old rose varieties only flower once a year, and they all flower at slightly different times depending on the climate their ancestors came from. This has the effect of staggering the main rose season over a period of about five weeks either side of a peak, which usually falls here around the longest day. Once the last flowers have finished, I remove the faded clusters with a pair of hand shears for speed, although repeat-flowering varieties would benefit from a more precise cut at the first leaf axil. There is a second, much smaller pulse of blooms in August thanks to the few old varieties that repeat flower and a selection from David Austin Roses. The latter are modern roses bred to preserve the same romantic flower shapes as the old ones but with repeat flowering and neater growth habits. While it is lovely to see the roses again in late summer, they seem oddly out of place. There is something inherently right about old roses in June: rather like snow at Christmas, it is this seasonal quality that makes the once-flowering varieties so enchanting.

> In their quest to attract pollinators, roses always aim to flower as high up as possible.

Right: Trained over metal domes, old roses 'Henri Martin' (on the left) and 'Gypsy Boy' grow as sturdy mounds smothered in flowers.

ROSE VARIETIES GROWING HERE

I took considerable time to research and choose which roses to grow and around three quarters of them are the true old-fashioned varieties, some of which have been in cultivation for over four hundred years. Key considerations were flower form and colour, plant height and habit, and most importantly they had to be robust, drought tolerant and disease resistant in order to cope with my hands-off gardening philosophy. Rose varieties fall into distinct families depending on their ancestry, and members of each group share similar characteristics, particularly in terms of growth habit and flowering times. Before we move on from the rose garden, let's take a closer look at some of my favourite varieties that grow here.

Rugosa hybrids

The rugosa hybrids are extremely hardy roses so they start into growth before the other rose families, as a result of which they are always the first to bloom here. They are enthusiastic repeat bloomers, often with three full flushes across the summer, and the flowers have some of the most intoxicating perfume in the whole rose garden. They produce stout, upright woody stems that can only be grown as freestanding bushes, and they are happy with little in the way of pruning except for the removal of dead wood in winter.

'Thérèse Bugnet' This lovely rose is unusually graceful for a rugosa hybrid as it has slender, arching stems. It forms a dense freestanding shrub about 2.2 m (7ft) tall and bears wide open double flowers in muddled shades of pink in two distinct flushes each summer.

Height and spread: 2.2 x 1.8m (7 x 6ft)
Suited to training: no
Early, middle, or late season: early
Repeat flowering: yes

'Martin Frobisher' A very hardy rose growing as a tall upright shrub with deep burgundy stems that contrast with very pretty pale pink flowers. The flowers are borne in three flushes each summer so that the bush is almost always in bloom.

> **Height and spread:** 1.8 x 1.2m (6 x 4ft)
> **Suited to training:** no
> **Early, middle, or late season:** early
> **Repeat flowering:** yes

'Roseraie de l'Haÿ' I treasure this rose for its scent, which is always such a surprise wafting from shaggy deep magenta flowers on an unremarkable woody-stemmed bush. It flowers here in two distinct flushes every summer and would be wonderful beside a path where the perfume can really be appreciated.

> **Height and spread:** 1.8 x 1.8m (6 x 6ft)
> **Suited to training:** no
> **Early, middle, or late season:** early
> **Repeat flowering:** yes

'Hunter' As the only truly red rose growing here, poor 'Hunter' has been relegated to a dead end so it doesn't clash with the pinks and magentas, but it is a wonderful short variety and its widely angled stems and suckering habit make a real impact. It flowers here in two full flushes, the second of which is often more impressive than the first.

> **Height and spread:** 1 x 1m (3 x 3ft)
> **Suited to training:** no
> **Early, middle, or late season:** middle
> **Repeat flowering:** yes

'Snowdon' This is one of my favourite roses and having earned its spurs in the rose garden, it features in the mirrored borders, too. Tall, strong, upright stems arch over at their very ends to create a handsome freestanding shrub that is completely smothered in clusters of double white flowers in three distinct flushes every summer. I can't recommend this variety highly enough.

> **Height and spread:** 2.2 x 1.8m (7 x 6ft)
> **Suited to training:** no
> **Early, middle, or late season:** early
> **Repeat flowering:** yes

'Belle Poitevine' An early flowering rose that makes a real impact with huge semi-double mid-pink flowers over wrinkled bright green leaves, and tall, strongly upright stems. It flowers twice here in two large flushes and the leaves flush bright yellow in autumn.

> **Height and spread:** 1.8 x 1.5m (6 x 5ft)
> **Suited to training:** no
> **Early, middle, or late season:** early
> **Repeat flowering:** yes

'Hansa' A wonderful rose that kicks off the rose season with large loosely double mid-magenta flowers in small clusters, and fills the surrounding air with the most enchanting perfume. It is rarely out of bloom all summer, and is often the first and the last variety in flower either side of the main rose season.

> **Height and spread:** 1.8 x 1.2m (6 x 4ft)
> **Suited to training:** no
> **Early, middle, or late season:** early
> **Repeat flowering:** yes

Bourbon roses

The Bourbon roses are remarkable and extremely healthy, tending to produce new stems in the second half of summer from higher up on old wood, so that they form a more enduring woody framework than most of the other rose families growing here. They flower quite early in the season and visually they are highly varied, producing some of the showiest blooms in the whole rose garden. You could easily create an entire rose garden with just Bourbons alone.

'Louise Odier' An elegant variety with flowers very like camellias, produced in clusters of 10 or so during the main flush and repeated in late summer at the tips of the new season's growth. It is trained over a very low metal dome here, but it would also be happy pruned as a freestanding shrub.

Height and spread: 1.6 x 1.2m (5 x 4ft)
Suited to training: yes
Early, middle, or late season: middle
Repeat flowering: yes

'Climbing Souvenir de la Malmaison' This rose is extremely robust and produces a wealth of new main stems in the second half of summer from rather complicated junctions on older wood. It is a joy to train along the wall where its span is impressive, and in warm dry weather the large flat, quartered flowers in palest powder pink are breathtaking. Sadly, the flowers ball very easily in wet weather, so despite its fabulous growth habit a good display is never guaranteed.

Height and spread: 4.5 x 3.5m (14 x 12ft)
Suited to training: yes
Early, middle, or late season: middle
Repeat flowering: no

'Blarii Number Two' A lovely climbing rose with brittle stems that need thoughtful handling, but the stunning two-tone pink flowers make it worth the effort.

> **Height and spread:** 3.5 x 2.5m (11 x 8ft)
> **Suited to training:** yes
> **Early, middle, or late season:** middle
> **Repeat flowering:** no

'Madame Lauriol de Barny' This rose is trained over a metal dome directly opposite the entrance gate to the rose garden, where it sets the tone for visitors with a stunning display of quartered double flowers that smother the entire dome and fill the air with perfume. The smooth stems would also be well suited to training around an obelisk.

> **Height and spread:** 2.2 x 1.2m (7 x 4ft)
> **Suited to training:** yes
> **Early, middle, or late season:** middle
> **Repeat flowering:** no

'Coupe d'Hébé' A very tall rose with clusters of globe-shaped mid-pink flowers that is well suited to training over a metal dome and would also be happy against a wall.

> **Height and spread:** 2.2 x 1.2m (7 x 4ft)
> **Suited to training:** yes
> **Early, middle, or late season:** middle
> **Repeat flowering:** no

'Gypsy Boy' This stunning rose has pride of place right in the centre of the rose garden, where I have wrangled a single shrub up through the centre of a metal dome and tied the stems horizontally around the outside. The individual blooms themselves are small pompoms that open rich magenta and pale to violet as they age, making each cluster a little work of art.

Height and spread: 1.8 x 1.2m (6 x 4ft)
Suited to training: no
Early, middle, or late season: middle
Repeat flowering: no

'**Honorine de Brabant**' Vigorous and very leafy, this rose is a curiosity for its striped pink and white flowers, and the overall effect is charming. It produces a wealth of new main stems every year, making it ideal for renewal pruning and training over a dome or around an obelisk.

> **Height and spread:** 1.8 x 1.8m (6 x 6ft)
> **Suited to training:** yes
> **Early, middle, or late season:** middle
> **Repeat flowering:** yes

'**Adam Messerich**' Tall and very slender, this rose is a real eyecatcher with loose, large-petalled flowers in a very bright mid-pink. It only produces a few stems and replacement growth is usually from higher up on old wood, but it is well worth growing with support.

> **Height and spread:** 1.8 x 1.2m (6 x 4ft)
> **Suited to training:** yes
> **Early, middle, or late season:** middle
> **Repeat flowering:** yes

Hybrid musks

These are wonderful roses and quite unlike the other rose families that grow here in both their habit and flower colours, which are mostly white, cream, and yellow. The stiff, self-supporting stems form large shrubs notable for their huge sprays of medium-sized flowers, both during their main bloom and again in autumn when the new season's growth terminates in further clusters.

'Buff Beauty' With smooth stems, red-flushed young leaves, and very large clusters of muted pale apricot flowers, this gorgeous rose forms a self-supporting woody shrub, but it can be coaxed around a support if required. New summer growth is topped with huge flower clusters in a second bloom in autumn.

Height and spread: 1.5 x 1.2m (5 x 4ft)
Suited to training: no
Early, middle, or late season: middle
Repeat flowering: yes

'Pax' A beautiful but unusual member of the hybrid musks in that it bears larger flowers in smaller clusters, but the creamy white petals opening from pointed buds are quite bewitching. It is very tall and rarely produces new stems from the base, making it well suited to training as a small climber.

> **Height and spread:** 2.2 x 1.2m (7 x 4ft)
> **Suited to training:** yes
> **Early, middle, or late season:** middle
> **Repeat flowering:** yes

'Prosperity' Growing in dry shade under the old oak tree by the greenhouse, this rose has really earned its spurs over the years. Despite the inhospitable site, it is covered in huge sprays of medium-sized pure white flowers in June and produces a good supply of new wood every year.

> **Height and spread:** 1.5 x 1.5m (5 x 5ft)
> **Suited to training:** no
> **Early, middle, or late season:** middle
> **Repeat flowering:** yes

Moss roses

The moss roses growing here are exceptional, producing strong, bendy, and extremely prickly new stems from the base every year that are very well suited to training over a support, although they would fan out along a wall equally well. The flower buds and stems are covered in mossy filaments that add a distinctive look to the plant both before and during flowering.

'Chapeau de Napoléon' This rose draws more attention for its fascinating crested buds than its classic mid-pink old-fashioned flowers, but the combination of the two make a real impact. While the tall, slender stems struggle to clothe their metal dome, it would be ideal for training around an obelisk.

Height and spread: 1.6 x 1.2m (5 x 4ft)
Suited to training: yes
Early, middle, or late season: late
Repeat flowering: no

'Henri Martin' This rose is astonishingly vigorous, producing so many long and pliable new stems from the base every year that almost all the old wood can be removed annually before the new growth is trained over its rose dome. In full bloom the velvety deep raspberry flowers are breathtaking, and it responds very well to being trained horizontally so the dome is completely smothered in flowers.

> **Height and spread:** 2.2 x 1.8m (7 x 6ft)
> **Suited to training:** yes
> **Early, middle, or late season:** middle
> **Repeat flowering:** no

'William Lobb' This rose also produces very long pliable stems every year from its base, some of which can reach 3m (10ft) in length, making them ideal for training along a wall, over a rose dome, or around an obelisk. The small clusters of crumpled flowers are charming, opening dark magenta and taking on violet tones as they age.

> **Height and spread:** 2.5 x 1.8m (8 x 6ft)
> **Suited to training:** yes
> **Early, middle, or late season:** late
> **Repeat flowering:** no

Alba roses

The albas are a graceful group of once-flowering roses with smaller flowers in shades of pink and white, and with a more restrained, slender growth habit that makes them well suited to life as a freestanding shrub.

'Celestial' A many-stemmed rose that forms a dense twiggy bush about 1.2m (4ft) tall, with grey-green leaves and small clusters of the most delicate pale pink flowers.

Height and spread: 1.2 x 1m (4 x 3ft)
Suited to training: no
Early, middle, or late season: late
Repeat flowering: no

'Königin von Dänemark' This strongly upright rose forms a slender shrub with three or four main stems, and bears long-lasting clusters of the most beautiful, flat, quartered flowers with a stunning perfume. It is very late blooming and often the last rose in flower at the end of the main season.

Height and spread: 1.5 x 1.2m (5 x 4ft)
Suited to training: no
Early, middle, or late season: late
Repeat flowering: no

'Alba Maxima' This ancient variety is a joy, producing clusters of double pure white flowers on a sturdy shrub with a good supply of replacement stems growing from low down on older wood.

Height and spread: 1.8 x 1.8m (6 x 6ft)
Suited to training: no
Early, middle, or late season: middle
Repeat flowering: no

'Maiden's Blush' This pretty rose forms a slender, strongly upright shrub about 1.5m (5ft) tall with just a few main stems, and bears clusters of small pale pink flowers that fade to almost white as they age.

> **Height and spread:** 1.5 x 1m (5 x 3ft)
> **Suited to training:** no
> **Early, middle, or late season:** late
> **Repeat flowering:** no

'Alba Semiplena' A slender-framed variety about 1.5m (5ft) tall with just a few main stems and simple, almost single pure white flowers with prominent golden centres.

> **Height and spread:** 1.5 x 1.2m (5 x 4ft)
> **Suited to training:** no
> **Early, middle, or late season:** middle
> **Repeat flowering:** no

Gallica roses

Gallicas are an absolute joy once you get the hang of them. Unusually for roses they produce numerous slender stems from near the base every year rather like raspberry canes, but if these are left long and without support they fall flat under the weight of their flowers. Some of mine are grown as freestanding shrubs with main stems cut to half their height, but gallicas really are spectacular if the full length of the stems can be trained and supported. They flower late in the rose season and include some of the deepest colours.

Rosa gallica* var. *officinalis This ancient rose is a real showstopper, producing clusters of bright magenta flowers with huge petals that pale as they age, giving the flower clusters a beautiful multitoned effect. It is grown as a freestanding shrub here and pruned to a manageable height, but the occasional stem that threads through the box ball behind blooms way above head height, so it could be much taller if given support.

> **Height and spread:** 1.5 x 1.2m (5 x 4ft)
> **Suited to training:** yes
> **Early, middle, or late season:** late
> **Repeat flowering:** no

'Président de Sèze' A lovely late-flowering variety that is pruned as a freestanding shrub here, but needs to be held back from the path when in full bloom due to the weight of the beautiful pink and mauve flowers.

> **Height and spread:** 1.2 x 1m (4 x 3ft)
> **Suited to training:** no
> **Early, middle, or late season:** late
> **Repeat flowering:** no

'Tuscany Superb' A stunning variety that produces a lot of pliable new stems from the base every year and covers its metal dome in clusters of deep claret flowers with prominent golden centres. The stems are not excessively long so this rose could easily be grown as a freestanding bush, but it would be very well suited to winding around a short obelisk.

> **Height and spread:** 1.5 x 1.2m (5 x 4ft)
> **Suited to training:** yes
> **Early, middle, or late season:** late
> **Repeat flowering:** no

'Charles de Mills' If I could have only one rose it would be this. The flat, quilled rosette flowers are astoundingly beautiful, opening a rich, deep foxglove colour that keeps its intensity as the flowers age. The slender stems also produce flower clusters all along their length when trained horizontally.

> **Height and spread:** 1.5 x 1.2m (5 x 4ft)
> **Suited to training:** yes
> **Early, middle, or late season:** late
> **Repeat flowering:** no

'Duchesse de Montebello' An unusually early pale pink-flowered gallica that forms a large arching shrub with a good supply of new growth from the base after flowering, and bears clusters of dainty rosettes with impossibly soft petals.

> **Height and spread:** 1.5 x 1.2m (5 x 4ft)
> **Suited to training:** yes
> **Early, middle, or late season:** middle
> **Repeat flowering:** no

Damask roses

These beautiful roses produce a lot of long, pliable new stems every year, making them ideal for growing over the metal domes where they are smothered in rosette-shaped flowers with petals like silk.

'Ispahan' This rose creates one of the most spectacular displays in the whole rose garden. The three plants growing by the rose garden wall are trained together over a metal dome that is smothered in long-lasting clusters of mid-pink flowers towards the end of the main rose season. After flowering, it produces a giddying number of extremely long, thin canes, making it completely impractical to grow as a freestanding bush, but it is worth any amount of trouble.

Height and spread: 2.2 x 1.5m (7 x 5ft)
Suited to training: yes
Early, middle, or late season: late
Repeat flowering: no

'La Ville de Bruxelles' A lovely rose with very prickly stems and unusually light green leaves that are a beautiful foil for the flat, quartered flowers in an attractive, uniform mid-pink. It produces a lot of strong, new growth every year, both from the base and higher up on old wood, making this rose well suited to training over a dome or around an obelisk.

> **Height and spread:** 1.5 x 1m (5 x 3ft)
> **Suited to training:** yes
> **Early, middle, or late season:** late
> **Repeat flowering:** no

'Madame Hardy' An elegant variety producing slender, pliable stems with clusters of flat pure white double flowers. It grows happily here with the stems arched over a ring of plant supports to create a small sturdy mound.

> **Height and spread:** 1.5 x 1.2m (5 x 4ft)
> **Suited to training:** yes
> **Early, middle, or late season:** middle
> **Repeat flowering:** no

David Austin varieties

These modern roses were bred to capture the charm of the old-fashioned flower shape without the challenging growth habit and once-flowering nature of the true old varieties. I decided to add some of them to the rose garden in the hope that together they would create a late summer flurry, but they really make their mark in the main rose season too.

'John Clare' An unobtrusive variety that grows here as a small, slender-framed bush with rather lax stems that happily mingle with surrounding plants. Once in flower, however, it is spellbinding, with rich mid-pink peony-like flowers that seem to have an inner glow. The flowers are borne in small clusters during the main season, and then in much larger clusters at the tips of the new season's growth in late summer.

Height and spread: 1.2 x 1m (4 x 3ft)
Suited to training: no
Early, middle, or late season: late
Repeat flowering: yes

'A Shropshire Lad' This variety dominates the rose garden wall where I have trained the stiff, thornless stems into a rather complicated lattice of old and new wood. The pale peachy pink flowers are archetypal old English roses and in full bloom the effect is enchanting. This large rose does not grow well here pruned short and the stems are stiff and unyielding, but it is perfect for training against a wall.

Height and spread: 2.5 x 2.2m (8 x 7ft)

Suited to training: yes

Early, middle, or late season: early

Repeat flowering: yes

'Constance Spry' Unusual for a David Austin rose, this variety flowers only once a year, but it is so magnificent in full bloom that I have it trained along the rose garden wall, over a metal dome, and also on the wall of the house. The blowsy old-fashioned flowers open sugar pink and fade as they age, and it produces a lot of very long, pliable new growth from the base every year, making it ideal for training in a variety of ways.

Height and spread: 3 x 2.5m (10 x 8ft)
Suited to training: yes
Early, middle, or late season: middle
Repeat flowering: no

'Mary Rose' This exceptional variety produces wave after wave of huge, double pink flowers, starting early in the main rose season and continuing until late autumn. It grows as a small, neat bush and is never chaotic in habit, even by the end of the season.

Height and spread: 1.2 x 1m (4 x 3ft)
Suited to training: no
Early, middle, or late season: early
Repeat flowering: yes

'The Alnwick Rose' The first thing that hits you about this rose is the stunning perfume: it reminds me of the scent of 'Albertine' and the pink flowers have the same hint of salmon to them. It grows as a very neat upright bush with stiff, thornless stems and a good supply of new wood every year.

Height and spread: 1.5 x 1m (5 x 3ft)
Suited to training: no
Early, middle, or late season: middle
Repeat flowering: yes

'Barbara Austin' Among the most beautiful in the whole rose garden, the flowers of this variety have the palest pink translucent petals, and a heavy perfume that more than makes up for the plant's thin stems and slender growth habit. Pruned as a freestanding bush, it tends to collapse under the weight of its flowers here, so I keep the full length of the stems and train them over a low metal dome where the effect is enchanting.

Height and spread: 1.2 x 1m (4 x 3ft)
Suited to training: yes
Early, middle, or late season: middle
Repeat flowering: yes

'Winchester Cathedral' Pure white flowers are borne in small clusters on this freestanding upright bush that grows well here pruned to 1m (3ft) tall. This variety is a sport (genetic mutation) of 'Mary Rose', and it has the same determination to flower right through until late autumn.

> **Height and spread:** 1.2 x 1m (4 x 3ft)
> **Suited to training:** no
> **Early, middle, or late season:** early
> **Repeat flowering:** yes

'The Mayflower' An unusually twiggy bush with intricate and beautiful flowers with downward-curving petals. The first flush is always the best, but it blooms sporadically across the summer with another main pulse of flowers here in August.

> **Height and spread:** 1.2 x 1m (4 x 3ft)
> **Suited to training:** no
> **Early, middle, or late season:** early
> **Repeat flowering:** yes

THE YELLOW GARDEN

Left: The simple layout and colour scheme create a relaxed and welcoming atmosphere.

We leave the rose garden through a metal arch flanked by columnar yew trees (*Taxus baccata* 'Fastigiata') set in a tall hedge and pass into the yellow garden. In contrast to the intensity and immersion of the rose garden, the yellow garden was conceived as a simple place to sit and read the paper, brush the dog, or just snooze in the sun. Since I started opening the garden for charity through the National Garden Scheme (NGS) in 2012, this area has rather morphed into a tea garden because it is the obvious place to set up the refreshments tent. The colour scheme here is simply yellows and whites because it is a corral for the yellow roses that I wanted to grow but not in line of sight of the colours in the rose garden. As the yellow garden is surrounded by hedges, it is a safe house for a colour that would clash with so many others in the view, and instead their burst of petal sunshine is welcome against the dark backdrop of yew.

Growing conditions vary widely here with dry shade under the laurels, damp shade on sticky orange clay by the beech hedge, and full to part-sun with good drainage elsewhere. Yellow rose varieties are mostly represented by hybrid musks and David Austin varieties together with some white-flowered albas, and the flowering perennials in shades of white and yellow include *Sisyrinchium striatum, Centaurea macrocephala, Digitalis lutea, Alchemilla mollis,* and *Phlomis russeliana.* There are two gravel hard standings set into the flowerbeds where *Geranium pratense* var. *pratense* f. *albiflorum, Digitalis purpurea* f. *albiflora, Alchemilla mollis,* and *Leucanthemum* x *superbum* happily self-sow and weave around the tables and chairs.

The yellow garden was laid out in September 2003 at the same time as the rose garden, and planting was completed in spring of 2004. Before work began, the site contained an enormous old hut and two mounds of flinty orange subsoil, and the beech hedge had not been trimmed for around 30 years. Once chopped to a sensible height, the lower trunks quickly bushed out, and a narrow path now forms the way out through a natural gap in between them.

THE PASTELS GARDEN

Right: Ox-eye daisies and later-flowering Campanula lactiflora *were quick to colonize any bare soil.*

Next on our tour we pass through the leafy tunnel between the beech trunks and out into the pastels garden. This is the only part of the garden in line of sight of the house. The site was already enclosed by the drive on the west side, the stable block and summerhouse to the south, the beech hedge to the north, and some mature native trees to the east (see the garden map on p.216). All these elements suggested a simple conventional layout with a large central lawn accessed by paths running through a ring of deep mixed borders. This layout means the beds have a definite front and back, and in order to square off the lawn they are all different depths, with the original planting six tiers deep in places. In easy reach of the house, a greenhouse sits on its own little gravel peninsula within the borders, surrounded by flowers and in every sense an integral part of the garden. The beds and paths for this area were laid out in the summer of 2004 and the initial planting started in that autumn.

Given the depth of the beds, I decided to experiment with some of the larger herbaceous perennials that I discovered while researching plants for the rose garden, and the beds were initially laid out in a precise fashion. Flower colours were blended like artists' pastels from blue through mauve to pink then white to yellow in waves and clusters around the garden, hence the garden's name. Very little conceptual thought went into the layout and design of the pastels garden so the result was pretty but uninspired, and it didn't have the distinct identity and subliminal triggers of the rose garden, or of the mirrored borders that were to follow. To give it a new sense of purpose, in 2013 I handed decision-making over to Mother Nature and it became an experiment in survival of the fittest, so everything growing here today has won its place in a feral community of crossing and self-sowing plants that thrive

> I handed decision-making over to Mother Nature and it became an experiment in survival of the fittest.

Above: Wild pink foxgloves soon crossed with the white strain to produce every shade in between.

Opposite: The beds are a fascinating mixture of the original planting and self-sown newcomers.

undisturbed. As nothing is watered, replaced, deadheaded, moved, or thinned, my role is restricted to weeding and clearing away the dead stems in winter.

Control of the appearance of these beds has been lost under the new regime, but they are lush and jostling with life even during heatwaves, and with every new generation, self-sown plants with a wider range of characteristics appear. Native wildflowers *Succisa pratensis*, *Origanum vulgare*, *Leucanthemum vulgare*, *Digitalis purpurea*, and *Knautia arvensis* now mingle with populations of *Geranium*, *Astrantia*, *Allium*, *Sisyrinchium*, *Epilobium*, *Eryngium*, *Sedum*, *Echinops*, *Camassia*, *Euphorbia*, *Campanula*, and *Thalictrum*. Exposing these beds to natural growing conditions has favoured earlier flowering species. These have time to flower and set seed before the harshest summer weather, and with later-flowering plants quickly crowded out by early starters in the battle for light and space, the peak season is earlier than it used to be.

THE MAGNOLIA WALK

Left: An explosion of magnolia petals in March heralds the end of winter.

The pastels garden is connected to the double mirrored borders by a long gravel path that runs all the way to the north boundary wall, where there is a stone bench surrounded by wisteria. The path is flanked by *Magnolia* x *loebneri* 'Leonard Messel', a pale pink-flowered variety that is slender and airy even when mature. There is nothing else in bloom to clash with the magnolia petals in spring, but in summer the colours here need to blend sensitively with the mirrored borders on one side and the distant rose garden on the other. This dictated the colour scheme, so plants here flower in shades of pale yellow and white, with a dash of purple and blue. The path edges are home to a self-sowing community of *Salvia verticillata*, *Cephalaria gigantea*, *Leucanthemum* x *superbum*, *Verbascum chaixii* 'Album', *Geranium pratense*, and *Centranthus ruber* 'Albus', with *Limonium platyphyllum* and the white-flowered *Allium cowanii* and *Allium nigrum* running alongside. Let us wander along the gravel path between the magnolia trees, and then take the little bark path near the stone bench that leads into the mirrored borders.

A TOUR OF THE GARDEN

THE MIRRORED BORDERS

Right: Staggered lines of evenly spaced Irish yew, obelisks, and box balls give form and structure to the borders.

This area of the garden was a scruffy field until 2008 and I used to sit on a bucket and stare at it for hours, trying to understand what it should become. It is 90 metres (300 feet) long and 18 metres (60 feet) wide, and a distinctly solitary place as it does not relate to anything except the huge expanse of sky. I didn't want to rob the space of its very stark and elemental character, so in the end I decided to marry the sky to the land by reflecting it down onto the ground through the colours and textures of the flowering plants. Taking this mirroring idea further, there are two lines of symmetry that run through the borders: one through the stone benches at either end and another through the wooden benches halfway along their length. This means that every plant appears four times, and as far as nature will allow, both sides and both ends are perfect mirrors of each other.

I decided to use geometry to emphasize the effects of perspective.

Unlike the rest of the garden, due to the strict symmetry of these beds no self-sowing is allowed, and because of this and the very restricted and precise colour scheme, I allowed myself to use named varieties to get the right shades of blue. My gardening philosophy still applies to these borders so they are managed in the same way as the rest of the garden, but as this was my last blank canvas, I wanted to try a different balance between the wild and cultivated elements within the design. By being more insistent about where things grow, the discipline and precision that underpin the whole garden are made visible on the ground.

Given the length of the borders, I decided to use geometry to emphasize the effects of perspective, so they are dominated by evenly spaced columnar yew trees (*Taxus baccata* 'Fastigiata'), white-painted obelisks, and clipped box balls (*Buxus sempervirens*). Bearded irises, clematis, and delphiniums define the journey along the length of the borders by starting at the far ends in the palest dawn-sky colours, and

then darkening in colour through sky-blue to deep midnight purples and blues at the halfway point behind the wooden benches.

Other plants that set the tone of the borders are *Erynigum, Sanguisorba, Echinops, Veronicastrum, Salvia, Aster, Artemisia, Sedum, Cynara cardunculus,* and *Hydrangea* 'Annabelle'. Except where it was necessary to use named varieties for precise control over the shades of blue, the herbaceous plants are all perennial species grown from seed or from divisions collected from elsewhere in the garden. Familiarity with the plants was very helpful in deciding what to grow here because the symmetrical design meant I had to be reasonably confident the plants would survive in all four locations. While the soil is poor and stony, the site runs north to south and growing conditions are quite uniform, so only a couple have struggled to establish in all four corners.

> The geometry and symmetry are dominant in the design and the colour scheme is strict, but within and around the discipline of these constraints there is a joyful dance of staggered rhythms and repeating and related motifs.

The borders are enclosed by a new brick wall that was built by a local contractor on rough grassland in the summer of 2008, and the stone benches at each end were assembled in that autumn, while the soil and seed for the lawn were laid in the spring of 2009. I finalized the planting plan in the winter of 2008/2009 so that planting could begin in early spring 2009, and it was finally complete by the spring of 2011.

If you stand at one end of the mirrored borders and walk across the lawn while looking down its length, the whole garden appears to swing around you in an optical illusion generated by the lines of perspective marked out by the box balls, obelisks, and yew trees. This reproduces an effect I observed while walking along the paths that cut through the nearby pine plantations, where the neat lines of the plantation trees generate the same illusion as you pass by, in striking contrast to the jumbled plant communities on the forest floor. The geometry and symmetry are dominant in the design and the colour scheme is strict, but within and around the discipline of these constraints there is a joyful dance of staggered rhythms and repeating and related motifs in an application of pattern-generating techniques that I extracted from listening to classical music on the radio. Where the rose garden is a reality pieced together from illusions, the mirrored borders are an illusion drawn from reality.

In contrast to the endless journey of the rose garden, the mirrored borders are built around the concept of destinations. As both ends and both sides are the same, there is no advantage to moving, and the hypnotic repetition, geometry, and perspective channel your focus on the far end to simultaneously lock your gaze and root you to the spot. The layout and design are also symbolic of my journey's end, as the drive that underpinned the garden's creation is finally brought to rest. Here, there are no new horizons, nothing just out of sight to lure you on, there is only the cycle of the sun and the seasons and total acceptance of containment in the here and now.

Myths and fairytales are densely woven into the fabric of this part of the garden. As an eternal hall of mirrors, a pool of reflections, it accommodates the Greek myth of Narcissus, Echo, and Nemesis. Icarus and Daedalus feature here too, with the lawn as a runway for Daedalus' escape from the maze of his own making and Icarus' demise showing the perils of flying on borrowed wings. Hans Christian Andersen's *The Little Mermaid* also finds expression here in the resolution of the conflict between being true to oneself and compromising to be accepted by others. This is a place where instinct and intellect work in harmony, where myths and maths contribute equally, and where by working together they bring the pursuit of illusion and its creation onto the same page. Where the rose garden explores the dynamic between the observer and the observed, the mirrored borders work to separate the creator from the creation and bring them face to face in a new and equal relationship.

> Myths and fairytales are densely woven into the fabric of this part of the garden.

Every area of the garden here is running its own experiments, and the rose garden and the mirrored borders are analogous to political systems. The dynamic free-for-all of the rose garden is like a liberal democracy: messy, competitive, highly adaptive and responsive to change, inventive, self-renewing, and ultimately healthy and joyous. In contrast the mirrored borders are like a dictatorship where nothing is up for discussion, nothing is allowed to innovate or evolve, and all decisions are made from the top. There is no role for self-sowing so the system sublimates the life drive, and in its place comes the tranquillity of transcending it. As with most dictatorships this is an increasingly vulnerable state of affairs, and unlike the ever-changing rose garden, the mirrored borders were predestined to fall victim to age and the changing climate in the longer term. Symmetry and precision bring a brittle quality to these borders that is a part of their identity: the tranquillity and constancy they embody are not part of nature's plan, but are instead the hard-won and easily lost consequence of discipline, control, and restraint.

Overleaf: In early June the mirrored borders are a counterbalance to the blowsy exuberance of the rose garden.

THE KITCHEN GARDEN

It is very hard to walk away from the tranquillity of the mirrored borders, but it is time to shake off their spell and stroll along the lawn to the little exit path at the south end. Here there is a white wooden gate that leads into a nursery area where plants are lined up for sale to garden visitors, and to the kitchen garden that runs in an L-shape around the outside of the mirrored borders' wall. The kitchen garden is about 100 metres (328 feet) long but never more than 11 metres (35 feet) wide. The dimensions result from its location on a margin of land set aside behind the mirrored borders' wall in order to use the east-facing side of the wall for training fruit trees. Despite the strange shape, it has been surprisingly easy to live with. Working down the far end does feel a bit like a day trip to the beach and there's no popping back and forth for things, but that is easily remedied by setting out with a carefully stocked wheelbarrow full of tools.

> My motto is: if it works eat it; if it doesn't learn from it.

Here I have been experimenting to find out what it takes to become self-sufficient in as much home-grown produce as possible, and all activities are designed as a quest for information rather than for specific results. I am not trying to win any prizes and every year I fully expect more than half of everything I grow to fail, so I am surprised and delighted when anything works and usually amused when it doesn't. My motto is: if it works eat it; if it doesn't learn from it. I use an old fridge as a cold store to keep apples and pears fresh through the winter, and I dry, pickle, or freeze the rest of the produce so seasonal gluts are available to eat in some form throughout the year.

Growing along the east-facing wall is a range of espaliered and fan-trained apple, pear, plum, cherry, peach, and apricot trees, and in the beds at the foot of the wall there are redcurrant, whitecurrant, and blackcurrant bushes. I also planted olive trees in between the long vegetable beds in anticipation of climate change, and at the

Above: Sweetcorn, sunflowers, and bread-seed poppies thrive near the south-facing side of the wall.

time of writing they are thriving and have even produced a handful of olives. When I first planted them in 2009, the long vegetable beds contained a five-bed rotation of legumes, brassicas, cucurbits, onions, and roots, but changes to spring weather here have made it increasingly hard for tender vegetables to establish, while the permanent fruit crops have proved very successful. Consequently, in 2022 I planted these beds with grape vines in the hope that they will be better suited to the climate in the years ahead. A further five smaller vegetable beds are still used for sweetcorn, winter squash, pumpkins, annual herbs, and sunflowers, as well as for a small stand of cobnut trees.

    I am sad to say that the kitchen garden marks the end of our tour, so I will leave you in peace to wander back through the mirrored borders and along the path between the magnolia trees. Take the curved narrow lawn that skirts the rose garden, and it will lead you to the wrought iron gate in the wall and back out onto the scruffy gravel drive. If I have done my job well, you will leave full of questions to which the rest of this book will provide the answers.

My nature-first gardening philosophy generated many challenges, and this chapter shares the observations, methods, and approaches I used to overcome them, while still maintaining a sensitive balance between the needs of the gardener and of the environment.

Chapter Three

GOING FERAL

Left: A profusion of self-sowing perennial species carpet the rose garden beds.

THE BEST OF BOTH WORLDS

Climate change and environmental concerns are on everyone's mind and we would all like to do our part, but there comes a point where the gut reaction says a particular sacrifice is just a step too far. Rewilding movements and concepts are motivated by pressing and vitally important concerns, yet if the process threatens the very gardenhood of a space then intuitively it will be met with resistance. Gardens are fulfilling in so many ways, and the impact of those different elements on our motivation really needs to be understood and respected if we are to feel our way successfully to a new balance between cultivation and wilderness.

This raises the question of what exactly is a garden? What is it about a space that defines it as a garden as opposed to a wild place? My own experience of studying views in nature that elicit an emotional response, and then translating them into a garden setting to trigger the same emotion, is very relevant because I spent a lot of time crossing the conceptual bridge between the two environments in the process.

What it boils down to for me is this: a garden should demonstrate evidence of a human hand, heart, and mind, whereas a wild place should demonstrate none of them.

> A garden should demonstrate evidence of a human hand, heart, and mind.

In conceiving the gardens here, I wanted to isolate and retain the key elements that trigger the feeling of gardenhood so they could be integrated into a place that actually functions as much like a wild environment as possible, and this turned out to be surprisingly easy to do. To get the best of both worlds, there are two things to consider: features that keep it looking like a garden on an intuitive level, and practices that allow it to operate like a wild place on a practical level.

Whether it is naturalistic or highly manicured, what really matters is that a garden shows clear evidence of a relationship between humans and a particular piece of earth. To feel like a garden on an intuitive level it needs visual evidence of a human hand, heart, and mind, and a hybrid between cultivated and wild needs to hold onto these visual cues or it will look neglected and feel distressing. Below are the elements that I used to disguise just how close to the wild my garden really is.

Focal points: with the exception of rainbows and waterfalls, natural environments do not throw up strong focal points but rather more diffuse compositions. A well-thought-out focal point seems to act like a shrine: it indicates that the spot is important to a human heart and its presence radiates intention and attachment.

Restricted colour schemes: I used this technique extensively in my garden for a variety of reasons, but what is key here is the way it instantly communicates thoughtful restraint. A planting scheme that would look like a chaotic wilderness in a wide range of colours appears mindful, deliberate, and highly disciplined when it has been established in a restricted colour scheme, but as far as nature is concerned, there is no difference between the two.

Geometry: geometry is found everywhere in nature, but usually on very small scales, such as in snowflakes and pine cones. Middle-sized geometric features seem to be a uniquely human affair, so they are a very good way to indicate human involvement.

Strong hard landscaping: with the eerie exception of basalt columns, Mother Nature is not prone to producing rocks with straight edges, so using them in hard landscaping is a sure sign of human handiwork.

Well-thought-out lines of sight and layout: between them these two elements infuse a garden with evidence of human thought, and the more decisive the lines of sight and routes around the garden are, the more they will act as a container for naturalistic chaos. Think of the impact of mowing a straight path through long grass or a wildflower meadow: that simple act transforms it from a wild place into something that instantly appears mindful and deliberate.

Livery: using the same plant supports, benches, paving slabs, brickwork, and so on all around the garden is a very effective way to create coherence and a distinct identity, as it works in the same way as a school uniform or a nation's street furniture. It also clearly demonstrates human thought, so is a very good trigger of gardenhood.

A few highly visible and highly manicured elements: every gardener knows the impact a freshly mown lawn and clipped edges can have on the look of an entire garden. It creates the impression that the whole place is tended with the same degree of precision, and that everything you see is therefore thoughtful and intentional. The

lawn is the most obvious example of this, but meticulously trained roses, clipped hedges, and box topiary have the same impact.

Absolutely no weeds: the simplest and most effective way to distinguish between a neglected garden and one that is being deliberately steered into a feral state in the interests of nature is the presence of weeds. The closer the approach is to nature, the more important it is to keep the garden scrupulously free of them, otherwise they will quickly take over and in a self-sowing regime they will be popping up everywhere.

Once these visual tricks are in place, there is a huge amount of room for welcoming natural systems into the garden without crossing the boundary into disenchantment, and when contained by the garden-making features, the feral qualities radiate a numinous charm that is often less apparent in a truly wild environment. Rather than letting a well-tended garden collapse into visual chaos on ethical grounds, bringing the two together thoughtfully brings out the best in both and increases emotional engagement with the garden. The following practices allow the garden to operate like a wild place.

> Allowing natural growing conditions to assert themselves is key to creating a self-sufficient and robust community of plants.

No interference in the growing conditions: the first in a chain of practices to establish wild systems in the garden is to allow natural growing conditions to reassert themselves. This means that the plants in the garden have to face the full force of the elements just as plants do in the wild, with no watering, no fertilizer, no protection from wind, heat, or cold, no deadheading, nothing added to the soil and nothing taken away, and only biological control of pests and diseases. Making the transition from a traditionally maintained garden to a feral one is going to involve some losses and this is the point in the process when they will occur, but it will be worth it: allowing natural growing conditions to assert themselves is key to creating a self-sufficient and robust community of plants.

Grow perennial species instead of named varieties: named varieties of plants are genetic clones that have often been deliberately bred for novelty or some particular visual feature. These are very far removed from Mother Nature's own species, which evolved as wild plants somewhere on Earth and have been shaped by natural selection to survive unaided for millennia. Growing seed-raised perennial species instead brings naturally occurring genetic diversity into the garden, and this is key if the plants are to be grown as populations that can adapt to a changing environment.

Left: Within this view, self-sown perennials are counterbalanced by a line of sight and focal point.

No deadheading: growing perennial species in natural conditions will set the garden up to harness natural selection by survival of the fittest, Mother Nature's tried and tested adaptation mechanism to steer the biosphere into alignment with the growing conditions. All that is needed now are the seeds to carry the survivors' genes from one generation into the next, so it is vital not to deadhead the flowers. Hundreds, even thousands of seeds are produced by each plant after flowering, and very few of them will even germinate let alone make it to maturity, so every one of those seeds counts and needs to make the journey back to the soil. Those that don't end up as the next generation of flowers will become part of the food chain in the garden, playing a part in the circle of life in one way or another.

Self-sowing: self-sown plants have grown without any input from the gardener at all, so they have already marked themselves out as survivors from the start. As they grow from open-pollinated seed they are all unique, so each one of them is a vital link in the process by which a species adapts to a new site. As the survivors cross with each other over the years, the garden will develop its own plant strains that are an imprint of the relationship between them and their environment, and these too will be unique to each garden. Just as in the wild, they are a living journal telling the history of the plant community and passing it on into the future.

Mingling plant populations not individuals: a healthy plant community in nature is one with a range of compatible species that grow in intermingled swathes or large neighbouring stands, and it contains self-sown plants at different stages of maturity, ensuring a healthy and sustainable future. Establishing this in the garden is a wonderful way to create a self-sustaining, healthy, wildlife-friendly environment, and a world away from a neatly dug flowerbed displaying individual specimens.

No bare soil: bare soil is anathema to nature and when it does occur, perhaps due to a burrowing animal or a fallen tree, it is only a matter of weeks before it is reclaimed by the biosphere like a wound healing over. Rather than striving for pampered specimens surrounded by a desert of bare soil, encouraging self-sowing ensures continuous shelter for the soil and for wildlife, while also creating gentler conditions for new seedlings to sprout.

Undisturbed plant communities: there is nothing more sobering in the countryside than the boundary between farmland and long-established woodland. On one side the land is stripped bare every year and left botanically impoverished with just dock and thistles for cover. The other side is the living consequence of generations of plants coexisting and adapting to each other and to the ever-changing environment, and this intricate interconnection would be lost if they were ever disturbed. I apply this lesson in the garden by ensuring the intermingled colonies of self-sowing plants are left in peace.

A wildlife park rather than a zoo: one of the ways I conceived of growing self-sowing perennial species was to think of the garden as a plant wildlife park rather than a zoo. In a zoo, animal species are segregated, given their own environment, and presented very much as isolated species with no sense of community. In a wildlife park, however, the focus is on populations in a shared environment, and they are regarded as much as possible as part of an integrated community within an overriding system that provides balance and continuity for all.

> Gardening with the health of the planet in mind requires a switch of focus towards protecting nature's systems.

Don't keep ailing plants alive: this goes against the instincts of many gardeners, but it is a vital part of welcoming natural selection into the garden. By letting ailing plants die, we are in effect replacing ourselves as the ultimate arbiter of what gets to live and die in our space. The desire to protect and nurture is of course natural when dealing with something we love, but the needs of one individual plant cannot take precedence over the interests of the population as a whole.

The health of the system takes priority over the individual: gardening with the health of the planet in mind requires a switch of focus towards protecting nature's systems rather than the individual plants within them. Establishing a self-sowing ecosystem in the garden means setting and keeping rules about what that system needs to function at its best, and where the interests of the system and the individual clash, this means investing emotionally in the health and needs of the system and always putting it first. This is something of a departure for many of us, however it is a small step along the way towards changing how we think about the planet-wide systems that affect us all.

These practices taken together effectively transform the garden into an ornamental ecosystem rather than a collection of plants, so let us take a look at this in more detail.

THE ORNAMENTAL ECOSYSTEM

The surrounding countryside is healthy, verdant, and dynamic with a rich and varied plant life, but no-one tends, waters, or fertilizes anything: it thrives precisely because it is constantly exposed to selection pressure rather than protected from it. As I began to understand the wild plant communities that live here, there was no way I could wander through them and return home convinced I was indispensable to the health of my garden. Instead, these communities made me realize that the more I restrain natural systems within my garden, the more I harm its natural vitality and adaptability, and the more dependent, vulnerable, and weak it becomes. This realisation encouraged me to garden with populations of perennial species, to allow my plants to live in as close to their natural state as possible, and to welcome and incorporate nature's systems into the garden so that the environment can prune out anything not suited to its spot and make room for something that is.

> Incorporating natural systems into the garden does not mean creating a garden that looks wild, merely one that lives by nature's rules.

I also realized that if plants and animals could coexist in the environment beyond my garden wall, then with the right gardening philosophy the same thing was possible inside the wall as well. I made it my policy to welcome all nature into the garden and not to focus on goodies and baddies, but instead to create a gardening system that mimics natural habitats as closely as possible in the hope that the same food chain and life cycles can take hold in my garden too.

As a result, gardening here is all about fitting in with the conditions as they are, and the ornamental ecosystem mimics how plants adapt to local conditions and fight it out between themselves in mixed communities in the wild. Thinking of the plants as self-sowing populations rather than individuals and exposing them to natural conditions means that the mature system contains only those plants that earn their spurs unaided. This may initially seem like giving up control, but it is quite the opposite: the approach is about accepting that I can never control everything in the garden, and then consciously focusing my efforts on the design of the system rather than firefighting on the ground. Careful attention to the colour scheme and scrupulous weeding along with the other elements described above maintain the reassuring look of a well-tended garden, so incorporating natural systems into the garden does not mean creating a garden that looks wild, merely one that lives by nature's rules.

Key to a thriving ornamental ecosystem is to allow each species to get enough seeds into the soil that they can find their own niches and set up communities with compatible neighbours. While they are adapting to the site and to each other, natural selection by survival of the fittest also ensures that the plant strains themselves adapt to the conditions of the site. This is something that can only happen in genetically diverse populations with subtly different characteristics that are fully exposed to the forces of nature with no interference.

The self-sowing understorey of perennial species in the rose garden has been managed in this way for over 20 years, and it is a thriving, dynamic, and endlessly inventive living system that exhibits the capacity to adapt to the changing climate and to self-heal from wounds thanks to the wealth of seeds in the soil. As in the wild, the understorey plants choose where they grow and adapt to conditions rather than being manacled to well-meaning but ultimately damaging assistance.

SETTING UP THE SELF-SOWING UNDERSTOREY
Establishing the self-sowing perennial understorey in the rose garden took three to five years, and was a rather chaotic process in its early stages as the plants found their way with the site and each other to reach a fully functioning system. I started by selecting a limited number of perennial species that were suitable for the location, seemed likely to be compatible with each other, and would create the right look and feel, while bearing in mind that they would be given free rein to pop up anywhere. I chose to use 12 different species and this has worked well: with too many the resulting mix would lack coherence and relatedness, but with too few it would lack interest and variety.

The perennial species I used in the rose garden were *Alchemilla mollis, Salvia verticillata, Phuopsis stylosa, Verbascum chaixii* 'Album', *Saponaria officinalis, Astrantia major, Campanula lactiflora, Echinops ritro, Echinops exaltatus, Centaurea montana, Valeriana officinalis,* and *Allium cristophii.* I also included native wildflowers, some grown from a seed pod collected on a local walk in the knowledge that they were already adapted to my conditions, and I am particularly fond of the naturally occurring white forms of native wildflowers as they add highlights to the tapestry of plants. Perennial wildflowers growing here include *Centranthus ruber* 'Albus', *Leucanthemum vulgare, Knautia arvensis, Succisa pratensis, Malva moschata, Geranium pratense* var. *pratense* f. *albiflorum, Epilobium angustifolium* 'Album', and *Teucrium scorodonia*.

I grew large numbers of seedlings in module trays and planted them out in drifts around the other plants where I thought they were most likely to thrive. This first generation were the only ones ever to be watered, and once established they were left to fend for themselves. Initial losses were high as was expected, and after a few years seedlings from the survivors began to appear around the parent plants, and then to colonize new areas where conditions were right for them. Plants don't have the option of moving their offspring away from unsuitable environments so they use a scattergun approach instead, creating a large and annually replenished source of genetic material. This makes open-pollinated plants primed to evolve and novel variations started to show up surprisingly quickly. From eight years onwards there was a visible increase in diversity between individual seedlings in terms of flower colour, flower size, flowering time, height, seed-setting propensity, and I suspect in responses to moisture levels and temperatures too.

> A frenzy of adaptation and evolution was in full swing behind the façade of a civilized and well-tended English country garden.

Once the understorey was fully established in the rose garden, things started to get very interesting. With no empty niches to colonize, new seedlings faced considerable competition to grow into adult plants. Populations began swirling around the rose garden like weather systems, and some that had died out on one side of the garden appeared years later on the other side, then seeded back to make a success of life in their original site. And all the while, any plant not suited to the conditions died out along the way. A frenzy of adaptation and evolution was in full swing behind the façade of a civilized and well-tended English country garden.

Using perennial species that live for many years seemed the best way to foster permanent plant communities, allowing them to establish and find their niche with each other gradually over time. This has worked very well. Unlike annuals that only get one chance to set seed, perennials get many chances to pass on their genes so a strong plant can dominate the gene pool across many generations. I added the biennial species *Eryngium giganteum* and *Digitalis purpurea* f. *albiflora* once the bedding-in process was almost complete to make sure they didn't hold it back, and they both now meander through the perennial carpet, popping up at random without disturbing the permanent plant communities at all.

Just as in nature the ornamental ecosystem revolves around seeds, and the strongest and best-placed plants will produce the most pollen, and then the most seedheads to take their success forward into future generations. For each species to colonize new territory, its propensity to set seed is key, as is its seed distribution mechanism and how long the seeds remain viable. Allowing all the seeds to accumulate in the soil creates a seed bank that functions as a memory of the battles lost and won by all the inhabitants of the garden. The mix of seeds in the soil also reflects the weather in previous years, as plants better suited to hot, dry conditions produce many more seeds after a long, hot summer than those preferring cool, moist conditions. It has been fascinating to see the impact of the previous year's weather on the type of seedlings that pop up the following spring, and a particularly good seed-setting year for any one species results in a boost to its population for several years to follow.

ADAPTING AN EXISTING FLOWERBED

I was working with a new garden so my experience of setting up an ornamental ecosystem was necessarily from scratch, but if you are interested in managing your garden in this way, then it should be very easy to adapt existing flowerbeds. The first thing to do is to stop watering, deadheading, fertilizing, dividing, mulching, and otherwise interfering with the plants already in place. This will flush out any plants that won't be able to survive under the new regime. Choose a selection of compatible perennial species to suit your conditions with the existing colour scheme in mind, grow them from seed, and set out the young plants in all the available space between the established ones. As the system matures and the plants mesh together, some existing plants will lose ground to the newcomers while others will join in and start self-sowing too. Seed-raised populations of perennial species are best placed to adapt to your site, but liberating the hidden genetic potential of named varieties is fascinating in its own right, and they have a lot to contribute if they are keen to self-sow. Keep on top of the weeds and over time your flowerbeds should develop into a healthy, self-sustaining tapestry that never needs watering and is full of variety, dynamism, and wildlife.

It is worth investing considerable time in drawing up a list of plant options because the better the fit with the conditions of your plot, the easier it will be to establish and the more varied and interesting your community of plants is likely to become over the long term. Undoing mistakes is not as straightforward as simply digging up a single pot-grown plant, as once you have released your choices into the garden, they could be popping up anywhere, so thoughtful planning will really pay off. It is very easy to discover online the native range and growing conditions of anything that catches your eye, and an image search will show you how the plant behaves in a wide range of real-life settings. In the next chapter I have provided as much information as I can about the

> Over time your flowerbeds should develop into a healthy, self-sustaining tapestry that never needs watering and is full of variety, dynamism, and wildlife.

perennial species that self-sow around the garden here, so if we garden in similar conditions (see climate information on p.216) this list would be a good place to start. Alongside internet searches and specialist seed catalogues, wildflower books covering your geographical region are also a useful source of ideas. To ensure you have enough variety in terms of height, growth habit, and flowering times, you will need at least 10 different perennial species, with a few more for luck as not everything will survive and thrive over time.

If sown in seed trays in early spring and then transplanted into module trays when large enough to handle, the seedlings should reach a suitable size for planting out in the garden by summer. Alternatively, with a late spring sowing they should be ready for planting out in autumn, when there will be no need to water them while they settle in. Plant them out in mingling drifts where they seem most likely to thrive, bearing in mind that they will be cross-pollinated by bees and other insects and seedlings could end up anywhere, so you are releasing them into a system rather than dictating where they will stay. It is very important not to water anything once the new plants are growing well, and in the first few years losses may be high, but this is all part of the plan as nature weeds out those that are not suited to their location or are not strong enough to hold onto their territory.

During this bedding-in process two different mechanisms are taking place: the strongest plants establish the largest crowns and dominate their communities, and self-sown seedlings slowly colonize bare soil and any empty spaces. If all goes well after three to five years, a continuous carpet should have formed with everything blended together.

> If I waded in with a watering can or deadheaded spent flowers it would undermine the whole process.

It is vital not to intervene during this period either by deadheading, watering, thinning, or mulching with anything other than fallen stems. The only exception is weeding, as Mother Nature would have it full of docks and nettles in no time if given an entirely free hand.

As the years go by and the community of plants knits together, there is less and less weeding to be done because seedlings of flowering plants fill every available space, and only a very determined nettle or bramble will take hold. In the early days however, there is a lot of bare soil, so careful weeding is essential to make sure weeds don't compete with the young perennials. The mix of seeds that builds up in the soil is what matters most, and my goal is to be able to take a tray of soil from the rose garden, add water, and have a miniature version of the understorey appear without

Left: Except for the shrubs and distant seed-raised delphiniums, everything in this photograph is entirely self-sown.

any weed seedlings. This is something that can only ever happen if weeds are never allowed to set seed. The other maintenance job is to cut down the dead stems during the winter months so that the display looks fresh and well tended the following spring. I leave the dead stems to rot down where they fall, and then rake off any large chunks that remain in early spring before the perennial crowns burst back into life and a new rash of seedlings germinates.

Setting up a self-sowing understorey with flowering perennial species is a wonderful way to fill your borders with pollinator-friendly flowers without compromising your commitment to the environment. Once established, it provides shelter and food for wildlife, the dense cover keeps the soil cool and moist in summer, and it allows your garden plants the right to choose where they live and the chance to evolve in lockstep with the changing climate.

A CHANGE OF PRIORITIES

It is only natural to be led into gardening by the beauty of flowers and to start a gardening project with a trip to the garden centre, returning home with a hefty bill and boot full of treasures. The ritual of choosing, bringing home, and planting these individuals is a considerable joy in itself, and it automatically skews concern towards their wellbeing. However, prioritizing the needs of the individual over the system endorses the use of gardening methods that damage the system where the two come into conflict. When focusing on the individual, the tendency is to regard the system as a threat to its success. In the garden this quickly translates into seeing other vital components of the ecosystem as bad guys that you need to act against to protect your chosen ones. If instead you are emotionally invested in the health of the system, this brings about a radical change of outlook, as without a chosen one there are no bad guys, there is no threat and no conflict, so you no longer feel motivated and justified to act in a way that damages the bigger picture. Encouraging evolving populations of plants in the garden is only possible if the needs of the system are given priority over the individual, as the mechanism of natural selection depends on it. If I waded in with a watering can or deadheaded spent flowers it would undermine the whole process.

Investing emotionally in the system rather than the individual plants within it turns a lot of gardening logic on its head, and this has implications for the values by which we judge ourselves as gardeners. When the health of the ecosystem is paramount then a plant infested with blackfly is no longer an innocent victim needing to be rescued, but rather an important host of food for blue tits and ladybirds. So many of the traditional conflicts in the garden vanish completely, and the drive to save one plant from the depredations of the surrounding ecosystem is shown for the harmful mission it really is.

When the plants are recast as components within an overarching system, their health, adaptability, robustness to disease and drought, and ability to coexist with their neighbours become far more important qualities than novelty, scarcity, or provenance. Death no longer becomes associated with failure, guilt, and disappointment. Instead, it becomes something fully anticipated and acknowledged as a healthy part of the system, and this changes your relationship with the garden. No longer a battleground where you win or lose in a fight to protect your chosen ones from the dark forces of the wild, the garden becomes an enchanted sanctuary where you and Mother Nature work quietly side by side towards a common goal.

> What we do in the garden will be contained by nature one way or another, so it makes sense to operate in the slipstream of natural processes rather than to fight them in a losing battle.

Growing plants as populations of a species rather than as individual named varieties also casts a more biologically accurate light on what information is relevant to their success. Populations of species don't need us to study the cultural identity we have projected onto them, they need us to study their own biological identity. They don't need us to keep one individual alive, they need us to allow them to self-sow and adapt to their environment as nature intended. In short, they don't need us to treat them like dependent mammals, they need us to respect the powerful survival mechanisms they evolved as plants.

It takes a while to adjust to the idea that a garden plant has to survive and thrive unaided and only then gains the right to pass on its genes, but adapting to a new balance of power in the garden mimics the change in our relationship with the planet. What we do in the garden will be contained by nature one way or another, so it makes sense to operate in the slipstream of natural processes rather than to fight them in what would be a losing battle. There is a profound peace that comes from working within nature's constraints, an elemental harmony that results from accepting diversity, chance, and loss as part of life: by letting go of the burden of trying to keep everything alive you can step back and celebrate the plants' triumphs rather than your own.

WELCOMING WILDLIFE

I consider wildlife to be as important to the garden as the plants, and I always act in a way that encourages a complete and self-regulating food chain in the garden rather than favouring any one part of it over another. The health of my plants depends on the creatures that live here in so many ways, and by managing the garden as an ornamental ecosystem the plants can return the favour and benefit wildlife in ways not possible in a traditionally maintained garden.

Allowing everything to set seed increases the available food in the garden and the number of birds and mammals it can support year-round. All those seeds are designed to survive over the winter and germinate in spring, making them a larder of stored energy available to tiny creatures during the leanest months of the year. Related to this is the garden's focus on pollinator-friendly flowers, as perennial species all evolved as wildflowers somewhere on earth and so they are ideally matched to the needs of pollinators. There are thousands of flowers around the garden, and with staggered blooming times they flower over a long period and provide a reliable food source for pollinators so they don't need to travel long distances. This is particularly helpful in late summer and early autumn when it improves their chances of making it through hibernation.

> My kitchen garden is something of a supermarket for the local wildlife, and there is always plenty left over for me.

The dense, leafy carpet that clothes the flowerbeds is ideal habitat for a wide range of wildlife, and in the rose garden they can cross the narrow paths from one bed to another without feeling exposed to predators. During the growing season I never see bare soil, and in place of a sun-baked desert there is a hidden world of tiny creatures living out their lives in cool, moist shade, burying seeds, eating slugs, and playing other vital roles in the food chain and life cycles of the garden. A big pile of old sticks makes wonderful habitat for all sorts of wildlife year-round, and I have sites hidden in each area of the garden where I take woody plant material to rot down. The piles are never disturbed so the oldest has been in place for over 20 years, and they create a reliable and accessible source of shelter that is particularly important in winter for insects and mammals.

I also allow birds and animals their share of the crops in the kitchen garden. I appreciate being able to do this depends on how much space you have to grow your own, but for me the bottom line is that I would rather feed the birds and animals than myself. Leaving redcurrants unnetted for the pigeons and blackbirds, growing sunflowers so chaffinches can prise out the seeds, watching the squirrels carry apricots along the top of the wall, growing globe artichokes so the bumblebees can dive headfirst into the violet filaments of their flowers, and growing sweetcorn in preparation for the local badgers' annual sweetcorn festival – all these bring me infinitely more joy than the crops themselves ever could. Rather than the scene of a battle against nature, my kitchen garden is something of a supermarket for the local wildlife, and there is always plenty left over for me.

There is nothing like stepping into someone's shoes to foster a newfound respect and admiration for their journey in life, and thinking anew about the creatures that live in the garden is a wonderful way to turn a problem on its head. If you are not plagued by pests but are instead being visited by respected guests, then providing them with food and shelter and clearing up after them becomes a joy. Underpinning this is an awareness that property rights are only designed to enforce territorial boundaries between humans. It might be my garden as opposed to another person's, but human property rights are not and never should be enforceable against another species. The creatures that live in my garden have just as much right to be here as I do, the garden is as much theirs as it is mine, and to stomp around complaining that I have badgers digging up my lawn is to confuse their territorial boundaries with my own.

It is important to remember that we are part of the ecosystem too. We have been at the top of the food chain for so long that it is easy to think of ourselves as set apart from it, but the things we do in the garden – from the plants we cause to grow to the materials we remove – are no different in essence from the actions of badgers, robins, or squirrels.

By replicating natural systems within the garden, by increasing the habitat and food the garden offers wildlife, and by tolerating the effects of their actions with a glad heart, my garden has built up a formidable food chain over the years and it is extremely rare that it gets out of balance. There are slugs, snails, aphids, spiders, butterflies and moths, wasps and bees, rabbits, badgers, foxes, hedgehogs, mice, bats, squirrels, hundreds of birds, and an army of tiny shrews that dart across the rose garden paths when I stumble out with my camera at sunrise. All these creatures have their roles to play in the garden, just as they do in the surrounding countryside.

Gardeners are often more familiar with growing annuals from seed than perennial species, but the process is very straightforward and during the growing season most hardy perennial seeds will germinate within three weeks if they are sown in a seed tray, kept moist, and left exposed to the elements. Once potted on, it takes a few months for the seedlings to grow large enough to be planted out in the garden and they rarely flower in their first year, but there are so many benefits for both the gardener and the garden that the patience required in the short term more than pays off.

Chapter Four

GROWING PERENNIAL SPECIES FROM SEED

Left: The natural variability of seed-raised perennials is part of their charm. This beautiful Astrantia major *seedling has pink-flushed flowers.*

WHY GROW PERENNIALS FROM SEED?

Right: Perennial species evolved within wild ecosystems, so they are natural magnets for pollinators.

The most obvious reason for growing from seed is the cost: hundreds of seedlings can be raised for the price of a single pot-grown plant, making even large-scale projects very affordable. In the early stages of setting up an ornamental ecosystem, plant losses can be high, and while this is a natural part of the process, it is much easier to take it in your stride when working with seedlings that cost pennies. Once you have decided on the perennial species for a project, there are usually numerous sources of seed online, but there is no guarantee that nurseries will have the plants ready and waiting in pots. Growing from seed therefore gives you more control over plant availability and ensures your project is not constrained by what plant suppliers have in stock.

As they can go on to live for many years, perennial seedlings are not programmed with the urgency to coordinate first-year flowering with each other, so unlike annuals, their seeds can be sown at any time during the growing season and they will still grow into healthy plants at a steady pace. On account of this, an early spring sowing will be ready to plant out in the garden in summer, a late spring sowing will be ready by autumn, and a late summer sowing will result in young plants that go dormant through the winter and burst back into growth the following spring.

Young perennials are relatively easy to transplant into their final positions and they settle in much faster and with less need for irrigation than fully grown ones. This quality is particularly valuable in a no-watering garden or when they are being planted out during the warmer months. Home-grown plants also have the advantage of spending their entire lives in the same garden, which makes the move into a flowerbed relatively stress free. In contrast, most perennials offered for sale in pots are much larger plants that have often been raised in artificial environments, and even those grown in garden-like conditions will still need to adjust to their new homes. To make matters worse they are often bought in full bloom, which is

completely the wrong time to plant them, and the combined stress can stop them from establishing well enough to survive their first winter in the ground.

All plants grown from open-pollinated seeds are genetically unique, so there will be natural variation in their characteristics. Gardeners have traditionally regarded this lack of uniformity in seed-raised perennials as a drawback, but when they are destined to live as self-sowing populations exposed to natural selection it becomes their greatest asset. As discussed in the previous chapter, this diversity means some plants will be better suited to the conditions in your plot than others. With time, the winners' seedlings have the potential to colonize every suitable niche in your garden, improving its health and resilience in the process.

> One of the most exciting things about gardening for me is discovering new perennial seedlings in the flowerbeds.

Genetically diverse plants also leave their mark on the look of a garden. There is an impressionist quality to my garden, which is in part the result of subtle variations within the populations of perennial species that grow here. Small differences in flower colour, height, size, and form merge with the effects of light and shade to create a dappled shimmer that is completely unobtainable with identical named varieties, or with plant collections where the difference between them is too great and introduces too much contrast.

One of the most exciting things about gardening for me is discovering new perennial seedlings in the flowerbeds. There is something about the feral nature of self-sowing that I find really fortifying, as if Mother Nature is right there gardening alongside me. It is vital that I can distinguish these tiny seedlings from weeds so I always sow seeds of unfamiliar plants in seed trays for the first time, just so I recognize their seedlings if they pop up in the garden.

Being involved in their journey from tiny seedlings all the way through to a fully established part of the garden fundamentally changes your relationship with the plants themselves, as it fosters a mindset of respect and nurturance rather than one of ownership and display. It is very easy to lose sight of their elemental character when layers of marketing, culture, commerce, and expense have wrapped themselves around your little plants. Growing from seed removes all these obstacles and leaves you with a profound sense of wonder that money just can't buy.

Caution Some plants and seeds are poisonous so always wear gloves when handling them and research their suitability if the safety of children and pets is a concern.

PERENNIAL SPECIES THAT SELF-SOW AROUND THE GARDEN

The following perennial species were initially grown here from seed and they now live in the garden as self-sowing populations. Some of them have established localized colonies, while others have spread far and wide and make a significant contribution to the garden's character. While every plot is a unique environment, this list makes a good place to start if you are investigating perennial species to add to your garden.

Alchemilla mollis A charming little plant which is a great foil for more eye-catching neighbours and acts as a link between surrounding flower and leaf colours. Its dew-spangled new growth in spring is as much a feature as the summer sprays of long-lasting flowers.

> **Height and spread:** 50 x 80cm (20 x 32in)
> **Growth habit:** sprawling plumes of tiny flowers over a mound of scalloped leaves.
> **Main flowering season:** June and July
> **Main flower colour:** acid yellow
> **Site and situation:** almost anywhere, but really thrives in well-drained part shade or sun. Not suited to waterlogged soil.
> **Good companions:** *Anthriscus sylvestris, Centaurea macrocephala, Digitalis lutea, Echinops ritro, Eryngium agavifolium, Eryngium giganteum, Geranium pratense* var. *pratense* f. *albiflorum, Phuopsis stylosa, Sedum spectabile, Sisyrinchium striatum, Teucrium scorodonia, Verbascum chaixii* 'Album'
> **Insect appeal:** moderate
> **Tendency to self-sow:** very high
> **Variability between seedlings:** low

Allium cristophii This magical allium sets the tone of the rose garden in spring and early summer. Self-sown colonies start out as leafy clumps in January when everything else is dormant and slowly mature into swathes of flowers like giant violet sparklers. They are all descended here from a bag of bulbs placed in the bottom of the sedum planting holes when the rose garden was laid out in 2004, and the cartwheeling seedheads have been spreading them around the rose garden ever since. First-year seedlings look just like chives, and the plants form a flowering-sized bulb after about three years.

> **Height and spread:** 60 x 30cm (24 x 12in)
> **Growth habit:** perennial bulb producing a leafy clump followed by huge globes of starry flowers.
> **Main flowering season:** May and June
> **Main flower colour:** metallic violet
> **Site and situation:** most sites, growing taller in shade. Not suited to growing through dense evergreen plants.
> **Good companions:** *Campanula persicifolia, Digitalis lutea, Eryngium bourgatii, Eryngium giganteum, Geranium pratense* var. *pratense* f. *albiflorum, Malva moschata, Phuopsis stylosa, Salvia verticillata, Sedum spectabile, Verbascum chaixii* 'Album'
> **Insect appeal:** high
> **Tendency to self-sow:** very high
> **Variability between seedlings:** high

Anthriscus sylvestris A local wildflower with delicate heads of lacy white flowers that transforms the country lanes in late spring. This short-lived plant is also a blessing in the garden, where it provides early-season height as it weaves between the leafy clumps of later-flowering perennials.

> **Height and spread:** 150 x 80cm (5 x 32in)
> **Growth habit:** flat, lacy flowers held on slender, upright ribbed stems.
> **Main flowering season:** May
> **Main flower colour:** white
> **Site and situation:** full sun or part shade with moist soil. Not suited to hot, dry sites and waterlogged soil.
> **Good companions:** *Allium cristophii, Campanula lactiflora, Centranthus ruber* 'Albus', *Digitalis lutea, Echinops ritro, Eryngium giganteum, Geranium sylvaticum, Leucanthemum* x *superbum, Phuopsis stylosa, Sedum spectabile, Teucrium scorodonia, Valeriana officinalis*
> **Insect appeal:** high
> **Tendency to self-sow:** high
> **Variability between seedlings:** low

Astrantia major This lovely clump-forming perennial has palmate leaves and magical pincushion flowers that are surrounded by green-flushed papery bracts. It tends to colonize the edge of flowerbeds and is an ideal choice for adding texture without too much colour.

Height and spread: 60 x 45cm (24 x 18in)
Growth habit: low, leafy mound with slender, upright flower stems.
Main flowering season: May to July
Main flower colour: green-flushed white
Site and situation: part or full shade beside a path or at the edge of a border. Not suited to hot, dry sites.
Good companions: *Anthriscus sylvestris, Campanula lactiflora, Campanula persicifolia, Digitalis lutea, Geranium pratense* var. *pratense* f. *albiflorum, Geranium sylvaticum, Saponaria officinalis, Succisa pratensis, Teucrium scorodonia, Thalictrum rochebruneanum, Valeriana officinalis, Verbascum chaixii* 'Album'
Insect appeal: high
Tendency to self-sow: high
Variability between seedlings: high

Camassia leichtlinii **'Alba'** Colonies of self-sown camassias kick off the main flowering season in the pastels garden in May and early June with graceful spires of creamy white flowers. The seedlings grow into single blades in their first year and take a few years to mature to flowering size, but they are well worth the wait.

Height and spread: 100 x 30cm (3¼ft x 1ft)
Growth habit: bulb producing a large, leafy clump in late winter followed by strongly upright flowers.
Main flowering season: May and June
Main flower colour: ivory white
Site and situation: a wide range of sites from damp shade to full sun. Not suited to waterlogged soil.
Good companions: *Campanula lactiflora, Centaurea macrocephala, Centaurea montana, Echinops ritro, Echinops sphaerocephalus, Epilobium angustifolium* 'Album', *Eryngium eburneum*
Insect appeal: moderate
Tendency to self-sow: high
Variability between seedlings: high

Campanula lactiflora This show-stopping plant is best suited to larger gardens. Young plants are quite short in their first few years, but once established the woody crown produces enormous stems topped with huge clouds of pale blue bells at head height.

Height and spread: 200 x 150cm (6½ x 5ft)
Growth habit: stout, unbranched leafy stems terminating in dense heads of small flowers.
Main flowering season: July
Main flower colour: pale blue
Site and situation: most sites, growing taller in damp shade and shorter in very dry soil. Not suited to path edges as it can flop when in full bloom.
Good companions: *Camassia leichtlinii* 'Alba', *Centaurea montana, Echinops ritro, Epilobium angustifolium* 'Album', *Geranium pratense* var. *pratense* f. *albiflorum, Phlomis russeliana, Sanguisorba tenuifolia* var. *alba, Sedum spectabile*
Insect appeal: high
Tendency to self-sow: high
Variability between seedlings: high

Campanula persicifolia A pretty little plant that forms a dense mat of dark green leaves, with slender upright stems bearing a succession of large harebell flowers at intervals along the stem. It tends to colonize the edges of beds and paths and mingles well with earlier-flowering plants of a similar habit.

> **Height and spread:** 40 x 20cm (16 x 8in)
> **Growth habit:** low, leafy mat with slender, upright flower stems.
> **Main flowering season:** June to July
> **Main flower colour:** blue
> **Site and situation:** edge of the border in shade or sun. Not suited to very hot, dry sites or tall neighbours.
> **Good companions:** *Allium cristophii, Centranthus ruber* 'Albus', *Eryngium giganteum, Eryngium planum, Geranium pratense* var. *pratense* f. *albiflorum, Geranium sylvaticum, Knautia arvensis, Limonium platyphyllum, Salvia nemorosa, Sisyrinchium striatum, Succisa pratensis*
> **Insect appeal:** moderate
> **Tendency to self-sow:** high
> **Variability between seedlings:** high

Centaurea macrocephala With donkey-ear leaves and stout leafy stems, this stocky plant bears impressive flower buds like ornate bronze bed knobs, which open into bright yellow filament flowers and then mature into thistledown seedheads.

> **Height and spread:** 150 x 80cm (5 x 2ft 8in)
> **Growth habit:** leafy unbranched flower stems from a basal clump.
> **Main flowering season:** July to August
> **Main flower colour:** yellow
> **Site and situation:** sun or shade in moist soil. Not suited to hot, dry sites.
> **Good companions:** *Alchemilla mollis, Anthriscus sylvestris, Astrantia major, Epilobium angustifolium* 'Album', *Leucanthemum* x *superbum, Phlomis russeliana, Sisyrinchium striatum, Valeriana officinalis*
> **Insect appeal:** moderate
> **Tendency to self-sow:** moderate
> **Variability between seedlings:** low

Centaurea montana This cheerful perennial cornflower is covered in large azure flowers with dark blue centres from late spring until early summer. Rather than mingle with other plants, it tends to dominate its spot, but the dense leafy block makes an attractive contrast.

Height and spread: 40 x 80cm (16 x 32in)
Growth habit: low, spreading leafy clump with sprawling flowering stems.
Main flowering season: April to June
Main flower colour: blue
Site and situation: most locations from full sun to damp shade. Not suited to shallow, stony soil.
Good companions: *Alchemilla mollis, Campanula lactiflora, Echinops ritro, Eryngium agavifolium, Eryngium eburneum, Geranium pratense* var. *pratense* f. *albiflorum, Knautia arvensis, Saponaria officinalis, Sisyrinchium striatum, Verbascum chaixii* 'Album'
Insect appeal: high
Tendency to self-sow: high
Variability between seedlings: moderate

***Centranthus ruber* 'Albus'** The pure white form of red valerian that grows wild on old walls, beaches and stony waste ground. Individual plants can be short lived, but once a population is established it pops up here and there, adding fluffy white highlights to the tapestry of flowers.

> **Height and spread:** 100 x 60cm (3¼ x 2ft)
> **Growth habit:** small leafy base producing long tiered plumes of tiny white flowers.
> **Main flowering season:** June and July
> **Main flower colour:** white
> **Site and situation:** hot, dry sites, poor stony or gravelly soil, seeding into walls and paths. Not suited to damp shade.
> **Good companions:** *Cephalaria gigantea, Cichorium intybus, Echinops ritro, Echinops sphaerocephalus, Eryngium giganteum, Geranium pratense* var. *pratense* f. *albiflorum, Knautia arvensis, Limonium platyphyllum, Malva moschata, Phlomis russeliana, Salvia verticillata, Sisyrinchium striatum, Verbascum chaixii* 'Album'
> **Insect appeal:** high
> **Tendency to self-sow:** high
> **Variability between seedlings:** low

Cephalaria gigantea An enchanting plant, ideal for weaving through a long view where its tall slender stems create a hazy screen. The pretty scabious flowers are held at head height, but the plant itself stays as a low leafy clump so it never blocks the view.

Height and spread: 200 x 50cm (6½ft x 20in)
Growth habit: low, leafy clump with tall, slender branching flower stems.
Main flowering season: June and July
Main flower colour: pale yellow
Site and situation: hot, dry, sunny sites, poor sandy and gravelly soil. Not suited to damp shade.
Good companions: *Cichorium intybus, Echinops ritro, Echinops sphaerocephalus, Eryngium agavifolium, Eryngium eburneum, Leucanthemum* x *superbum, Limonium platyphyllum, Phlomis russeliana, Salvia verticillata, Sanguisorba tenuifolia* var. *alba, Sisyrinchium striatum, Verbascum chaixii* 'Album'
Insect appeal: high
Tendency to self-sow: high
Variability between seedlings: low

Cichorium intybus A naturalized European wildflower that is perfectly adapted to hot dry sites and very poor soil. From a neat leafy clump, it produces strongly upright slender branching stems that bear soft blue dandelion flowers over a long period in high summer.

Height and spread: 120 x 60cm (4 x 2ft)
Growth habit: low, leafy clump with slender, upright branching flower stems.
Main flowering season: July and August
Main flower colour: pale blue
Site and situation: poor soil, hot, dry sites, sun-baked areas where nothing else will grow. Not suited to damp shade.
Good companions: *Centranthus ruber* 'Albus', *Cephalaria gigantea, Cynara cardunculus, Eryngium bourgatii, Eryngium eburneum, Limonium platyphyllum, Salvia nemorosa, Salvia verticillata, Sisyrinchium striatum*
Insect appeal: high
Tendency to self-sow: high
Variability between seedlings: low

Cynara cardunculus The handsome and architectural cardoon grows in several sites around the garden, where it contributes a striking clump of jagged silvery leaves in late winter, enormous branching stems with ornate thistle flowers in August, and an explosion of thistledown in early autumn. A single mature plant can anchor a long view or create a centrepiece in a large border.

Height and spread: 2.4 x 1.8m (8 x 6ft)
Growth habit: stout, branching stems towering above a clump of enormous silvery leaves.
Main flowering season: August
Main flower colour: violet
Site and situation: hot, dry sites in full sun or partial shade, poor soil. Not suited to full shade or strong winds, small gardens or confined spaces.
Good companions: *Allium cristophii, Camassia lechtlinii* 'Alba'*, Campanula lactiflora, Echinops ritro, Epilobium angustifolium* 'Album'*, Phuopsis stylosa, Salvia verticillata, Sanguisorba tenuifolia* var. *alba, Succisa pratensis*
Insect appeal: very high
Tendency to self-sow: moderate
Variability between seedlings: low

Digitalis lutea An elegant perennial foxglove with small, pale-yellow flowers and shiny, dark green leaves that makes an ideal contrast to neighbouring plants with brighter flowers and looser outlines.

Height and spread: 100 x 50cm (3¼ft x 20in)
Growth habit: neat, leafy clump with upright flowering stems.
Main flowering season: June to July
Main flower colour: pale yellow
Site and situation: part shade, weaving through densely planted areas. Not suited to hot, dry sites.
Good companions: *Alchemilla mollis, Allium cristophii, Anthriscus sylvestris, Campanula persicifolia, Eryngium giganteum, Geranium pratense* var. *pratense* f. *albiflorum, Knautia arvensis, Leucanthemum* x *superbum, Limonium platyphyllum, Phuopsis stylosa, Salvia verticillata, Sisyrinchium striatum, Teucrium scorodonia*
Insect appeal: moderate
Tendency to self-sow: moderate
Variability between seedlings: low

Digitalis purpurea* f. *albiflora The white-flowered form of our native wild foxglove, this biennial plant pops up all over the garden adding a touch of grace wherever it goes. Self-sown seedlings form an overwintering rosette in their first year and then extend central flowering stems with the first warm days of spring to bloom from the end of May until early July. Individual plants die after setting seed, so it is important to make sure all the seeds are in the soil before clearing old stems away or the population will die out.

> **Height and spread:** 200 x 40cm (6½ft x 16in)
> **Growth habit:** tall, flowering wands rising from leafy rosettes.
> **Main flowering season:** May to July
> **Main flower colour:** white
> **Site and situation:** most sites, but happiest in a mixed perennial tapestry in dappled light. Not suited to hot, dry sites.
> **Good companions:** *Allium cristophii, Campanula lactiflora, Centaurea montana, Eryngium giganteum, Geranium pratense* var. *pratense* f. *albiflorum, Geranium sylvaticum, Sedum spectabile, Succisa pratensis, Teucrium scorodonia, Valeriana officinalis*
> **Insect appeal:** very high
> **Tendency to self-sow:** very high
> **Variability between seedlings:** high

Echinacea purpurea A lovely little herbaceous perennial that sits as a neat leafy clump through early summer and then produces large daisy flowers with domed centres in high summer.

> **Height and spread:** 60 x 40cm (24 x 16in)
> **Growth habit:** low, leafy clump with strongly upright flower stems.
> **Main flowering season:** July and August
> **Main flower colour:** mauve pink
> **Site and situation:** happy here in shade and moist soil in full sun. Not suited to dry, sun-baked soil.
> **Good companions:** *Allium cristophii, Astrantia major, Eryngium eburneum, Eryngium giganteum, Geranium pratense* var. *pratense* f. *albiflorum, Knautia arvensis, Limonium platyphyllum, Phuopsis stylosa, Succisa pratensis, Teucrium scorodonia*
> **Insect appeal:** high
> **Tendency to self-sow:** moderate
> **Variability between seedlings:** high

Echinops ritro A striking globe thistle with stout, upright leafy stems topped with spiky geometric flower buds that soften under a bloom of tiny pale blue flowers.

> **Height and spread:** 140 x 60cm (4½ x 2ft)
> **Growth habit:** branching flower stems above a large leafy clump.
> **Main flowering season:** July to August
> **Main flower colour:** blue
> **Site and situation:** part shade to full sun. Not suited to damp shade.
> **Good companions:** *Anthriscus sylvestris, Alchemilla mollis, Campanula lactiflora, Centranthus ruber* 'Albus', *Cephalaria gigantea, Phlomis russeliana, Phuopsis stylosa, Salvia nemorosa, Salvia verticillata, Sanguisorba tenuifolia* var. *alba, Saponaria officinalis, Sedum spectabile*
> **Insect appeal:** high
> **Tendency to self-sow:** high
> **Variability between seedlings:** low

Echinops sphaerocephalus A very modest and accommodating globe thistle that is ideal for smaller gardens or a more restricted space, where its branching silvery stems and geometric flowers contribute texture without taking over.

Height and spread: 100 x 60cm (3¼ x 2ft)
Growth habit: stout, branching flower stems rising from a low, leafy clump.
Main flowering season: August
Main flower colour: white
Site and situation: full sun and tolerant of dry soil. Not suited to full shade and permanently damp soil.
Good companions: *Campanula lactiflora, Centaurea montana, Centranthus ruber* 'Albus', *Cephalaria gigantea, Cichorium intybus, Epilobium angustifolium* 'Album', *Eryngium agavifolium, Eryngium eburneum, Limonium platyphyllum, Sisyrinchium striatum, Succisa pratensis, Verbascum chaixii* 'Album'
Insect appeal: high
Tendency to self-sow: high
Variability between seedlings: low

***Epilobium (Chamaenerion) angustifolium*
'Album'** This white-flowered form of wild rosebay willowherb never looks out of place owing to its mesmerizing beauty. It spreads underground on long white roots so you never quite know where the shoots will turn up each year, but the individual stems are very happy to mingle with neighbouring plants.

Height and spread: 180 x 300cm (6 x 10ft), but each flowering stem is only 20cm (8in) wide
Growth habit: slender, leafy flowering stems from an underground network of roots.
Main flowering season: July to August
Main flower colour: white
Site and situation: large densely planted borders where it can come and go without consequence. Not suited to small gardens, precisely planned flowerbeds, or hot, dry sites.
Good companions: *Alchemilla mollis, Campanula lactiflora, Centaurea macrocephala, Echinops ritro, Echinops sphaerocephalus, Eryngium eburneum, Leucanthemum* x *superbum, Sanguisorba tenuifolia* var. *alba, Sedum spectabile*
Insect appeal: moderate
Tendency to self-sow: low
Variability between seedlings: low

Erynigum agavifolium A handsome architectural plant that forms an evergreen clump of spiny leaves with smooth upright flower stems topped with clusters of green-tinged white drumstick flowers.

Height and spread: 150 x 80cm (5ft x 32in)
Growth habit: evergreen, leafy clump with strong, upright flowering stems.
Main flowering season: July and August
Main flower colour: green-white
Site and situation: full or part sun and tolerates dry, stony soil. Not suited to damp shade.
Good companions: *Alchemilla mollis, Allium cristophii, Centranthus ruber* 'Albus', *Knautia arvensis, Limonium platyphyllum, Malva moschata, Salvia verticillata, Sisyrinchium striatum, Succisa pratensis, Verbascum chaixii* 'Album'
Insect appeal: high
Tendency to self-sow: moderate
Variability between seedlings: moderate

Eryngium bourgatii The archetypal blue sea holly with spiky bracts, drumstick flowerheads, and smooth stems, all flushed with metallic blue. This plant has a very deep taproot, and it starts and ends the growing season as an attractive clump of silver-veined leaves.

> **Height and spread:** 40 x 50cm (16 x 20in)
> **Growth habit:** low, sprawling clump.
> **Main flowering season:** June and July
> **Main flower colour:** blue
> **Site and situation:** hot, dry sites, poor soil, the edge of patios. Not suited to damp shade.
> **Good companions:** *Centranthus ruber* 'Albus', *Leucanthemum* x *superbum*, *Limonium platyphyllum*, *Salvia nemorosa*, *Sanguisorba tenuifolia* var. *alba*, *Sedum spectabile*, *Verbascum chaixii* 'Album'
> **Insect appeal:** high
> **Tendency to self-sow:** moderate
> **Variability between seedlings:** moderate

Eryngium eburneum An elegant evergreen sea holly that makes a significant contribution to the garden through its form and texture, as well as providing a foil for more colourful neighbours. The slender upright stems bear tiny egg-shaped flowerheads on numerous stalks radiating from a single point, giving the whole plant a candelabra-like appearance.

> **Height and spread:** 150 x 80cm (5 x 32in)
> **Growth habit:** evergreen, clump of strappy leaves with smooth branching flower stems.
> **Main flowering season:** July and August
> **Main flower colour:** white
> **Site and situation:** full sun and tolerates poor soil. Not suited to damp shade.
> **Good companions:** *Anthriscus sylvestris*, *Campanula lactiflora*, *Centaurea macrocephala*, *Cephalaria gigantea*, *Cichorium intybus*, *Echinops ritro*, *Epilobium angustifolium* 'Album', *Geranium pratense* var. *pratense* f. *albiflorum*, *Limonium platyphyllum*, *Sanguisorba tenuifolia* var. *alba*, *Verbascum chaixii* 'Album'
> **Insect appeal:** high
> **Tendency to self-sow:** high
> **Variability between seedlings:** moderate

Eryngium giganteum This remarkable plant charts the course of summer in the rose garden, with stout flowering stems that emerge from leafy clumps in June, mature into branching silver bracts in July, and then finally turn rich golden brown in late August. They grow very long taproots so prefer to be direct sown rather than raised in trays and pots, and each individual plant dies after setting seed so it is very important to make sure the seeds have fallen into the soil before clearing the stems away, otherwise the population will quickly die out. This plant is a real treasure in high summer when the bracts add refreshing architectural highlights to the tapestry of flowers and maturing seedheads.

> **Height and spread:** 70 x 40cm (28 x 16in)
> **Growth habit:** low clump of bright green leaves with a single stout, upright stem branching into spiky, silver bracts.
> **Main flowering season:** July to August
> **Main flower colour:** silver-white
> **Site and situation:** full to part sun in dry or moderately damp soil. Not suited to inflexible planting schemes, deep shade, or permanently damp soil.
> **Good companions:** *Alchemilla mollis, Allium cristophii, Campanula persicifolia, Centranthus ruber* 'Albus', *Digitalis lutea, Echinacea purpurea, Phuopsis stylosa, Salvia verticillata, Sedum spectabile, Valeriana officinalis, Verbascum chaixii* 'Album'
> **Insect appeal:** high
> **Tendency to self-sow:** high
> **Variability between seedlings:** moderate

Eryngium planum A later-flowering blue sea holly ideal for mixing with earlier blooming plants, where the slender upright stems weave through neighbours and transform tired borders with swarms of little metallic blue domes surrounded by decorative bracts.

> **Height and spread:** 120 x 30cm (4 x 1ft)
> **Growth habit:** small, leafy base producing very slender, upright flower stems.
> **Main flowering season:** July and August
> **Main flower colour:** blue
> **Site and situation:** part to full sun, tolerates poor and gravelly soil. Not suited to damp, shady locations.
> **Good companions:** *Anthriscus sylvestris, Campanula lactiflora, Centrathus ruber* 'Albus', *Digitalis lutea, Echinops ritro, Geranium pratense* var. *pratense* f. *albiflorum, Geranium sylvaticum, Knautia arvensis, Leucanthemum* x *superbum, Succisa pratensis, Valeriana officinalis*
> **Insect appeal:** very high
> **Tendency to self-sow:** high
> **Variability between seedlings:** low

Geranium pratense* var. *pratense* f. *albiflorum The white form of wild meadow cranesbill, this pretty plant pops up all around the rose garden where it adds soft white crests to the tapestry of flowers.

Height and spread: 90 x 60cm (3 x 2ft)
Growth habit: mound of palmate leaves below slender, branching flower stems.
Main flowering season: June
Main flower colour: white
Site and situation: weaving through dense planting, full or part sun. Not suited to deep shade, and grows shorter in hot, dry locations.
Good companions: *Allium cristophii, Centaurea montana, Digitalis lutea, Echinops ritro, Eryngium giganteum, Malva moschata, Phuopsis stylosa, Salvia verticillata, Sedum spectabile, Sisyrinchium striatum, Valeriana officinalis, Verbascum chaixii* 'Album'
Insect appeal: very high
Tendency to self-sow: very high
Variability between seedlings: high

Geranium sylvaticum This delicate early-flowering geranium adds a welcome splash of colour in between the leafy clumps of later-blooming neighbours.

Height and spread: 50 x 40cm (20 x 16in)
Growth habit: neat, leafy clump with slender stems bearing small clusters of single flowers.
Main flowering season: April to May
Main flower colour: blue, pink, or white
Site and situation: sun or part shade in a dense tapestry of plants. Not suited to sun-baked, poor soil.
Good companions: *Astrantia major, Campanula persicifolia, Eryngium eburneum, Sedum spectabile, Sisyrinchium striatum, Succisa pratensis, Teucrium scorodonia, Thalictrum rochebruneanum, Valeriana officinalis*
Insect appeal: high
Tendency to self-sow: very high
Variability between seedlings: very high

Leucanthemum* x *superbum An indispensable plant that looks like a giant ox-eye daisy, but it flowers much later in the summer and some seedlings can reach a considerable height. Superb for freshening up the borders in high summer, when a few plants dotted through earlier-flowering neighbours can transform the view.

> **Height and spread:** 80 x 70cm (32 x 28in)
> **Growth habit:** low, dense leafy mat producing numerous upright flowering stems.
> **Main flowering season:** July to August
> **Main flower colour:** white
> **Site and situation:** dry or moist soil in full sun or part shade. Not suited to dry shade where it will sprawl.
> **Good companions:** *Alchemilla mollis, Centaurea macrocephala, Cichorium intybus, Echinops ritro, Echinops sphaerocephalus, Epilobium angustifolium* 'Album', *Eryngium eburneum, Eryngium planum, Geranium pratense* var. *pratense* f. *albiflorum, Limonium platyphyllum, Phlomis russeliana, Phuopsis stylosa, Sanguisorba tenuifolia* var. *alba, Sisyrinchium striatum*
> **Insect appeal:** moderate
> **Tendency to self-sow:** very high
> **Variability between seedlings:** high

Knautia arvensis A beautiful local wildflower that grows beside the country lanes with pale lavender buttons on long slender stems held above clumps of soft felty leaves.

Height and spread: 80 x 70cm (32 x 28in)
Growth habit: dense, leafy mound with slender, branching flower stems.
Main flowering season: May to July
Main flower colour: pale lavender
Site and situation: poor stony or chalky soil, but thrives in most conditions. Not suited to deep shade and permanently wet soil.
Good companions: *Allium cristophii, Campanula persicifolia, Campanula lactiflora, Centranthus ruber* 'Albus', *Geranium pratense* var. *pratense* f. *albiflorum, Leucanthemum* x *superbum, Phuopsis stylosa, Succisa pratensis, Verbascum chaixii* 'Album'
Insect appeal: very high
Tendency to self-sow: high
Variability between seedlings: moderate

Limonium platyphyllum This charming little plant forms a low clump of leathery leaves with very branching wiry stems studded with hundreds of tiny violet flowers in high summer.

Height and spread: 70 x 50cm (28 x 20in)
Growth habit: leafy clump with branching wiry flower stems.
Main flowering season: July and August
Main flower colour: violet
Site and situation: dry sites and poor soil, full sun to partial shade. Not suited to damp, shady sites.
Good companions: *Allium cristophii, Centranthus ruber* 'Albus', *Cephalaria gigantea, Cichorium intybus, Salvia verticillata, Sanguisorba tenuifolia* var. *alba, Sisyrinchium striatum, Succisa pratensis, Verbascum chaixii* 'Album'
Insect appeal: moderate
Tendency to self-sow: moderate
Variability between seedlings: moderate

Malva moschata A pretty wildflower often seen as a flash of pink by the roadside, this plucky little plant can cope with hot, dry, poor soil and will also weave through a dense tapestry of plants. Clusters of medium-sized single flowers are borne at intervals along the end section of the stems. It can be short lived, but adds most to the garden when it pops up unexpectedly here and there.

Height and spread: 80 x 60cm (32 x 24in)
Growth habit: sparse, leafy stems growing from a single point.
Main flowering season: July
Main flower colour: pink
Site and situation: cracks in paths and patios, the edge of beds, and any bare soil between other plants. Not suited to deep shade.
Good companions: *Centranthus ruber* 'Albus', *Echinacea purpurea, Echinops ritro, Echinops sphaerocephalus, Eryngium agavifolium, Eryngium giganteum, Eryngium planum, Geranium pratense* var. *pratense* f. *albiflorum, Limonium platyphyllum, Salvia nemorosa, Salvia verticillata, Teucrium scorodonia, Valeriana officinalis*
Insect appeal: high
Tendency to self-sow: high
Variability between seedlings: low

Phlomis russeliana A completely weed-proof plant that forms a dense mat of rooted stems with large felty leaves that persist right through the winter to be replaced by new growth in spring. Upright stems are produced in early summer, whorled with tiers of pale yellow flowers and followed by domed seedheads that are very popular here with chaffinches.

Height and spread: 70cm (28in) x indefinite
Growth habit: dense mat of rooted stems with year-round leaf cover and upright flower stems.
Main flowering season: June
Main flower colour: yellow
Site and situation: virtually anywhere but particularly useful in dry poor soil and full sun. Not suited to a small space: this is a carpeting plant on a mission.
Good companions: *Alchemilla mollis, Campanula lactiflora, Cephalaria gigantea, Echinops ritro, Epilobium angustifolium* 'Album', *Leucanthemum* x *superbum, Sanguisorba tenuifolia* var. *alba*
Insect appeal: moderate
Tendency to self-sow: very high
Variability between seedlings: low

Phuopsis stylosa This delightful groundcover plant quickly spreads to clothe bare soil with a dense, weed-proof mat of mossy leaves studded with gorgeous fluffy pink flowers in early summer. It is ideal for scrambling between shrubs and under roses, has a gift for knitting together a self-sowing perennial understorey, and stays leafy and verdant right through until early winter.

Height and spread: 30cm (12in) x indefinite
Growth habit: low, mat-forming plant with mossy leaves.
Main flowering season: June
Main flower colour: pink
Site and situation: covering large areas of ground in a wide range of conditions. Not suited to full shade or permanently damp soil.
Good companions: *Alchemilla mollis, Allium cristophii, Campanula lactiflora, Eryngium eburneum, Eryngium giganteum, Geranium pratense* var. *pratense* f. *albiflorum, Knautia arvensis, Malva moschata, Saponaria officinalis, Salvia verticillata, Sedum spectabile, Teucrium scorodonia, Verbascum chaixii* 'Album'
Insect appeal: moderate
Tendency to self-sow: high
Variability between seedlings: moderate

Salvia nemorosa A tough and long-lived plant with slender tapering stems bearing deep blue trumpet flowers above felty leaves.

> **Height and spread:** 80 x 60cm (32 x 24in)
> **Growth habit:** loosely upright, leafy branching stems from a single point.
> **Main flowering season:** July and August
> **Main flower colour:** blue
> **Site and situation:** hot, dry sites, full to part sun. Not suited to damp shade.
> **Good companions:** *Campanula persicifolia, Centranthus ruber* 'Albus', *Echinacea purpurea, Echinops ritro, Eryngium eburneum, Eryngium planum, Knautia arvensis, Leucanthemum* x *superbum, Limonium platyphyllum, Malva moschata, Sedum spectabile, Succisa pratensis*
> **Insect appeal:** high
> **Tendency to self-sow:** high
> **Variability between seedlings:** low

Salvia verticillata A cheerful little plant that tends to grow at the front of flowerbeds and beside paths, where its lax leafy stems and muted purple bracts and flowers soften outlines and blend with a wide range of neighbours.

Height and spread: 40 x 70cm (16 x 28in)
Growth habit: sprawling mound of leafy stems.
Main flowering season: July and August
Main flower colour: purple
Site and situation: full sun and poor soil, self-sows into gravel paths. Not suited to deep shade and very damp soil.
Good companions: *Allium cristophii, Centranthus ruber* 'Albus', *Cephalaria gigantea, Digitalis lutea, Eryngium giganteum, Knautia arvensis, Sedum spectabile, Succisa pratensis, Verbascum chaixii* 'Album'
Insect appeal: high
Tendency to self-sow: high
Variability between seedlings: moderate

Sanguisorba tenuifolia* var. *alba This magnificent plant forms a dense woody crown with a low clump of attractive ferny leaves. Then in late summer tall slender wands of fluffy white catkin flowers transform the view just when the other plants are looking tired. It mixes well with a wide range of perennial species and the ferny leaves are an attractive foil for neighbouring plants through the summer months.

> **Height and spread:** 240 x 80cm (7¾ft x 32in)
> **Growth habit:** low, leafy clump with tall, slender flowering stems.
> **Main flowering season:** August and September
> **Main flower colour:** white
> **Site and situation:** a wide range of conditions from full sun to full shade, self-sows into gravel paths and worth a try anywhere.
> **Good companions:** *Anthriscus sylvestris, Camassia leichtlinii* 'Alba', *Campanula lactiflora, Echinops ritro, Echinops sphaerocephalus, Eryngium bourgatii, Eryngium eburneum, Phlomis russeliana, Salvia verticillata, Saponaria officinalis, Sedum spectabile, Valeriana officinalis, Verbascum chaixii* 'Album'
> **Insect appeal:** moderate
> **Tendency to self-sow:** high
> **Variability between seedlings:** high

Saponaria officinalis A leafy carpeting plant that forms a weed-proof colony and transforms into a bank of soft pink phlox-like flowers in late summer. It spreads far and wide so is ideal anywhere a large area of low-maintenance leaf and flower is needed.

Height and spread: 50cm (20in) x indefinite
Growth habit: upright to lax leafy stems terminating in panicles of single flowers.
Main flowering season: July and August
Main flower colour: pink
Site and situation: thrives in all conditions. Not suited to small areas as it tends to form very large colonies.
Good companions: *Astrantia major, Campanula lactiflora, Centaurea montana, Echinops ritro, Eryngium giganteum*
Insect appeal: moderate
Tendency to self-sow: moderate
Variability between seedlings: moderate

Sedum (Hylotelephium) spectabile This cheerful plant has something to contribute from April all the way through to October. The tight, fleshy-leaved shoots are a joy in spring, and it grows into a neat rounded mound between summer-flowering neighbours before taking centre stage to flower in September and October. It is very long lived and spreads by both seed and fallen stem sections, so it tends to colonize areas near to the original plant.

Height and spread: 80 x 60cm (32 x 24in)
Growth habit: tight rounded clumps of fleshy, pale green leaves followed by flat flowerheads in autumn.
Main flowering season: late September and October
Main flower colour: muted pink
Site and situation: most conditions, but more lax in damp, shady sites. Not suited to waterlogged soil.
Good companions: *Alchemilla mollis, Allium cristophii, Anthriscus sylvestris, Echinops ritro, Echinops sphaerocephalus, Eryngium giganteum, Geranium pratense* var. *pratense* f. *albiflorum, Phuopsis stylosa, Salvia nemorosa, Succisa pratensis, Thalictrum rochebruneanum, Valeriana officinalis, Verbascum chaixii* 'Album'
Insect appeal: high
Tendency to self-sow: moderate
Variability between seedlings: low

Silene uniflora This pretty wildflower grows as a dense spreading carpet of grey-green leaves covered in white flowers for a long period in summer. A native of coastal locations, it is very happy self-sowing into the gravel here.

> **Height and spread:** 20 x 70cm (8 x 28in)
> **Growth habit:** low, spreading mat-forming plant.
> **Main flowering season:** June and July
> **Main flower colour:** white
> **Site and situation:** full sun and stony or gravelly soil. Not suited to damp soil in full shade.
> **Good companions:** C*entranthus ruber* 'Albus', *Digitalis lutea, Geranium pratense* var. *pratense* f. *albiflorum, Leucanthemum* x *superbum, Limonium platyphyllum, Sisyrinchium striatum, Succisa pratensis*
> **Insect appeal:** moderate
> **Tendency to self-sow:** high
> **Variability between seedlings:** low

Sisyrinchium striatum A charming little plant easily mistaken for an iris until slender upright stems appear that are studded with clusters of small pale yellow flowers. It copes with most conditions here and likes to self-sow beside paths and patios.

> **Height and spread:** 60 x 40cm (24 x 16in)
> **Growth habit:** clusters of leafy fans with slender, upright flower stems.
> **Main flowering season:** June
> **Main flower colour:** pale yellow
> **Site and situation:** gravel, stony soil, patios, and path edges. Not suited to deep borders or damp shade.
> **Good companions:** *Alchemilla mollis, Campanula persicifolia, Centaurea macrocephala, Centranthus ruber* 'Albus', *Cephalaria gigantea, Cichorium intybus, Digitalis lutea, Echinops ritro, Eryngium agavifolium, Eryngium eburneum, Geranium pratense* var. *pratense* f. *albiflorum, Knautia arvensis, Limonium platyphyllum*
> **Insect appeal:** moderate
> **Tendency to self-sow:** very high
> **Variability between seedlings:** low

Succisa pratensis A delightful local wildflower that sits as a neat dark green leafy clump until the end of summer, and then produces a mass of slender wiry stems bearing small button flowers until early autumn.

Height and spread: 80 x 70cm (32 x 28in)
Growth habit: small, leafy clump with long, slender flowering stems.
Main flowering season: August and September
Main flower colour: purple-blue
Site and situation: most conditions. Not suited to sun-baked, shallow soil.
Good companions: *Campanula persicifolia, Eryngium eburneum, Eryngium giganteum, Knautia arvensis, Leucanthemum* x *superbum, Limonium platyphyllum, Salvia nemorosa, Sanguisorba tenuifolia* var. *alba, Sedum spectabile, Verbascum chaixii* 'Album'
Insect appeal: very high
Tendency to self-sow: high
Variability between seedlings: very high

Teucrium scorodonia This understated wildflower first caught my attention in the local woods with its wrinkled leaves and tiny pale yellow trumpet flowers, and it has proved a worthy component of the perennial understorey in the rose garden. It has established around the base of a couple of the roses and mingles happily with neighbouring plants.

Height and spread: 40 x 40cm (16 x 16in)
Growth habit: small, leafy base with slender, tapering flower stems.
Main flowering season: July and August
Main flower colour: very pale yellow
Site and situation: mixing with other low perennials in full sun or part shade. Not suited to hot, dry sites.
Good companions: *Alchemilla mollis, Astrantia major, Echinacea purpurea, Eryngium bourgatii, Eryngium eburneum, Eryngium giganteum, Knautia arvensis, Limonium platyphyllum, Malva moschata, Phuopsis stylosa, Succisa pratensis, Valeriana officinalis*
Insect appeal: high
Tendency to self-sow: moderate
Variability between seedlings: low

Thalictrum rochebruneanum An extremely elegant plant with slender upright stems clasped at intervals by maidenhair-fern-like leaves and topped with loose panicles of tiny pendent flowers like miniature anemones.

> **Height and spread:** 200 x 40cm (6½ft x 16in)
> **Growth habit:** slender stems rising from a neat, leafy clump.
> **Main flowering season:** June to July
> **Main flower colour:** pale violet
> **Site and situation:** moist soil in part or full shade. Not suited to hot, dry sites where the growing points will shrivel in early summer.
> **Good companions:** *Anthriscus sylvestris, Astrantia major, Geranium pratense* var. *pratense* f. *albiflorum, Geranium sylvaticum, Knautia arvensis, Phuopsis stylosa, Sanguisorba tenuifolia* var. *alba, Valeriana officinalis, Verbascum chaixii* 'Album'
> **Insect appeal:** moderate
> **Tendency to self-sow:** moderate
> **Variability between seedlings:** low

Valeriana officinalis A graceful and very fragrant plant that mingles well with a wide range of self-sowing perennials owing to its very slender growth habit. The tall narrow stems hold clusters of tiny, pink-tinged white flowers well above the tapestry of plants below, adding hazy highlights to the view.

Height and spread: 180 x 60cm (6 x 2ft)
Growth habit: small, leafy base producing very tall, upright flower stems.
Main flowering season: late June to August
Main flower colour: white
Site and situation: mingling with neighbouring plants in light shade or part sun. Not suited to hot, sun-baked sites.
Good companions: *Alchemilla mollis, Anthriscus sylvestris, Astrantia major, Echinops ritro, Eryngium agavifolium, Eryngium giganteum, Leucanthemum* x *superbum, Sedum spectabile, Teucrium scorodonia, Verbascum chaixii* 'Album'
Insect appeal: high
Tendency to self-sow: high
Variability between seedlings: low

***Verbascum chaixii* 'Album'** A long-lived plant that forms a neat clump of large, wrinkled leaves and produces slender spires of small white flowers with fluffy, mauve-pink centres that bloom over a long period in high summer. The strongly vertical flowering stems are very effective spearing up through mound-forming plants and beside paths.

Height and spread: 90 x 40cm (3ft x 16in)
Growth habit: leafy clumps with strongly upright flowering stems.
Main flowering season: June and July
Main flower colour: white
Site and situation: most conditions, tolerating hot, dry sites but growing much larger in moist soil.
Good companions: *Alchemilla mollis, Allium cristophii, Astrantia major, Campanula lactiflora, Centaurea montana, Eryngium giganteum, Geranium pratense* var. *pratense* f. *albiflorum, Malva moschata, Sedum spectabile, Thalictrum rochebruneanum, Valeriana officinalis*
Insect appeal: very high
Tendency to self-sow: high
Variability between seedlings: moderate

Visitors to my garden often comment on its very elemental feel, and they are particularly struck by the way it captures the spirit of the surrounding countryside. In this chapter I share some observations drawn from using the countryside as the primary source of design ideas, together with a more in-depth explanation of how scale and the concepts of journey and destination influenced my design choices. I also share observations drawn from photographing the garden, and some comments on finding your own unique garden style.

Chapter Five

DESIGN OBSERVATIONS

Left: Farmland on the flat hilltop affords an uninterrupted view of wide open sky.

DESIGN OBSERVATIONS

THE COUNTRYSIDE AS A SOURCE OF DESIGN IDEAS

Right: Curved paths in the local woods add a sense of mystery and adventure to the view.

Gardens have the power to trigger instincts and emotions that can blend into a sense of wonder, anticipation, and enchantment on a very intuitive level. It is no surprise that this is also true of natural environments as for most of human history we lived alongside untamed countryside, and I am quite sure the experience is a legacy of our old way of life being stirred to the surface. To examine this more closely, I spent time walking in the surrounding lanes and woodlands studying my own emotional responses to different aspects of the countryside. I then teased out which features I could use to trigger the same reactions in my garden, and these are described below.

Narrow transitions: passing between two different environments in the countryside is a very intense experience when the transition is a tiny gap in the hedge as opposed to an open gate with far-reaching views. This inspired me to create narrow transitions from one area of the garden to another to heighten the sense of anticipation and adventure.

Three storeys of planting: key to capturing the feeling of walking in the woods are the different storeys of trees, shrubs, and herbaceous plants that make up deciduous woodland. The tall canopy provides dappled shade and containment for the bigger picture, the middle storey comprises shrubs and small trees such as yew, holly, hazel, and hawthorn, and the ground is carpeted with mixed colonies of perennial wildflowers and grasses. I used this three-storeys approach to give the rose garden an enchanted woodland feel.

> I really don't acknowledge a distinction between wildflowers and garden plants.

The wide-open sky: it is impossible to ignore the sky at Bladbean. The hamlet is on the flat top of a hill, and the horizon seems to fall away in every direction, giving the sky a dominance that weighs almost palpably on the land. This elemental and inescapable feature is fundamental to the design of the mirrored borders.

Curved paths: numerous narrow trails run through the local woods, and where a section of the path ahead is curved, it is a very powerful trigger for anticipation, suspense, and adventure because the way is clear but the destination is obscured. Each step reveals a new section of the path while at the same time changing your angle in relation to the surroundings, and this generates a sequence of different alignments and views along the way. This effect is an important part of the rose garden's design.

Repeating tiers and layers: running alongside the local country lanes, the verges are rich and varied habitats that are enchanting visually when they stretch away into the distance in repeating tiers and layers. At 90 metres long and 5 metres wide (300 feet by 17 feet), the mirrored borders were designed to be viewed along their length rather than at right angles to the lawn, and ideas gleaned from the verges were key to creating an effective planting scheme for them.

Wildflowers: the diversity, subtlety, and grace of wildflowers and how they mingle with each other influenced my choice of plants for the garden. As a consequence, I really don't acknowledge a distinction between wildflowers and garden plants. Indeed, by growing perennial species instead of named varieties, almost every perennial here is a wildflower that evolved somewhere on Earth. Local wildflowers are given equal prominence in the garden, and some were even grown from a seed pod collected on a walk, so the resulting population of plants is from a long line of survivors on this hilltop.

Successional planting within fixed roles: I love the way rosebay willowherb takes over the role of the fading foxgloves, how wild angelica blooms after common hogweed – which in turn follows the cow parsley – and how hawkbit steps in when the dandelions are over. Hawthorn blossom follows the blackthorn in spring, and in the nearby nature reserve, common orchids, then fragrant, and then pyramidal orchids bloom in succession across the longest days of the year. The way these similar-looking flowers hand the baton to each other gives the landscape an enduring identity, while at the same time marking the passing of the seasons as nature intended. This gave me the idea of using a succession of plants to take over fixed roles from each other within the planting scheme for the mirrored borders.

Enchanted glades: there is nothing quite as breathtaking and memorable as coming around a corner in the woods and stumbling across an enchanted glade, maybe with a shaft of sunlight on a patch of foxgloves, or a group of wild angelica sparkling with dewdrops. While the focal point is riveting, these experiences are mostly the result of the approach, framing, backdrop, and restriction of surrounding views, and I used this knowledge throughout the garden as a matter of course.

Mass planting and a restricted range of plants: one of the defining characteristics of a location in the countryside is what grows there, and over the years I have built up an extensive mental map of where all the different plants can be found on my walks. Usually, a restricted number of compatible species grow in mixed colonies and sometimes they grow alone in large stands, and this gives a distinct identity to each place. I used this effect extensively in the garden by giving different areas their own localized populations of plants to enhance the sense that they are distinct places from each other.

Immersion: the experience of walking through the woods on narrow trails creates a feeling of immersion and the sense of being contained within a greater living system that stretches away in all directions, except for the axis you are travelling along. While this limits choices and visibility, it does so in a soothing and benevolent way. I used this effect extensively in the rose garden where the paths cut through planting that often towers above head height, creating the experience of being part of the garden rather than just an observer of it.

SCALE, JOURNEY, AND DESTINATION

One aspect of walking in the countryside that stood out as particularly relevant to designing a garden was the impact of the scale of a space on what seemed to matter about it. I responded very differently to my surroundings depending on their scale, and in a large space my most pressing questions seemed to be about how to travel through it. Where is the path? Which is the best route? How do I get to the other side? This implies that a design that emphasizes journey using strong lines of sight, perspective, repeating motifs, dominant paths, and route markers would be the most effective for a large area, as it would resonate most closely with our instinctive interest in it.

> For a small garden to be effective, it needs to feel like a credible destination.

A small space, however, needs to be rewarding in a very different way, as my instinctive reaction was always the same. Should I stop here? What gives me the sense of having arrived at this point rather than any other? Do I feel safe to be off guard here? This suggests that for a small garden to be effective, it needs to feel like a credible destination, with not just a comfortable place to sit but also a strong sense of enclosure. Everything needs to be visible from every vantage point so that the drive to explore is replaced with a profound sense of peace and focus, generating a secure and contemplative place where it feels safe to relax and be off guard.

The scale of a space also dictates the distance from which its contents will be viewed, and this has implications for the most effective choice of plants. In a small courtyard, every detail will be visible wherever you stand, so planting in ones and twos while emphasizing the variety and intricacy of individual plants will be very effective. If the space is large, however, then everything will be viewed from a distance so individual plants will appear almost as tiny pixels. In this case it makes sense to approach the design as if painting a landscape, and to use plants that are good sources of colour and texture en masse. Making decisions about what to plant where from a distance will help to ensure the patches are in the right proportions within the view, rather than being too small to make an impact.

> One of the easiest ways to stitch large views together is with repetition of a restricted range of plants.

Key to creating a unified overall picture in a large space is the way plants relate to each other, and one of the easiest ways to stitch large views together is with repetition of a restricted range of plants. Not only does this guarantee balance with simultaneous blooming spread over the whole area, but it also gives the garden a distinct identity in the same way that different locations have their own plant communities in nature. A visual journey can be created very easily in a large space by using repetition alone, and when the same plant appears in the foreground, middle-, and background along a line of sight, it also highlights the impact of perspective to give an instant impression of both journey and distance.

If the plot is so big that using relatedness and a journey won't be enough to tie the garden together, it can instead be turned into a succession of separate areas, each with its own character. To trigger anticipation there needs to be enough screening between the different areas so that they are obscured from each other. Narrow transitions between them will also intensify the experience of leaving one and crossing into the next. I structured the whole garden here around this type of layout, and the rose garden in itself is also designed to capture something of this effect, with a maze of crossing paths filling it with glades and vistas always hidden out of sight around the next corner.

Despite the large scale of the space, the mirrored borders were designed to contain features of a journey and a destination combined. The repeating structural elements and matching plants near and far create a visual journey along the length of the borders. Meanwhile everything is visible at once from every vantage point, there is a strong sense of enclosure, and both ends and both sides are the same with four secure and relaxing places to sit. It is as though a single destination has been split and pulled apart to create an environment that feels both safe and free at the same time. While the layout channels attention with intense focus onto a single point at the far end, the magnetic draw of the destination is counterbalanced by its mirror image behind you, holding the drive to move towards either horizon in stasis.

Having first studied my responses to scale, journey, and destination in the countryside, I chose the layout of the rose garden and the mirrored borders knowing the instincts they trigger would work to amplify their purpose. Walking around the rose garden was intended to be an immersive sensory cornucopia for our ancient gathering instincts, and the layout of the mirrored borders was designed to engage and contain hunter-like focus, assisted by a colour scheme in shades of blue and white that removes all other distractions and merges into the sky.

THROUGH THE LENS

I studied my reactions to the surrounding countryside to work out the designs for the garden, but through the process of taking daily photographs of the garden since 2015 I have inadvertently been studying the garden itself in a similar way. This has brought some interesting observations to light that could be applied to other gardens.

A formula for signature views: over the years I have noticed that photographs of certain views act as the garden's calling card, and it is striking that they all follow the same formula of a distant focal point with a dark backdrop and a valley-shaped visual journey towards it.

Curved versus straight paths: taking photographs of curved and straight paths through the growing season has really demonstrated the different qualities they bring to the view. The hypnotic focus of a straight path is commanding and confident, and everything either side of it appears to be in the service of whatever lies at its end. Curved paths, however, have an entirely different character as they create a playful and beguiling mystery. Views with curved paths always have a fairytale quality about them as if they lead to a land far far away, and in a sense they do, as they leave room for the imagination to fill in what lies just out of sight.

Repeating motifs: my focus on repeating motifs such as box balls, yew columns, and plant supports when designing the garden was mostly an attempt to give it a

Opposite: Sunlit cardoon leaves and shaded Artemisia *create a fleeting visual journey.*

distinct identity by creating its own livery. It has become apparent through the photographs that the power of these motifs to stitch views together is also very pronounced, as they appear to call to each other over very large distances and create a visual journey of their own.

Bare soil: bare soil completely destroys any photograph it appears in as it looks and feels like a wound on Mother Earth. Outside the mirrored borders, the garden was designed to be clothed in a continuous tapestry of perennial plants so it is very rare that I come across bare soil while taking photographs. When I do, however, the visual and emotional impact is stark and jarring.

White: occupying a strange hinterland in the garden, white doesn't behave like a colour but rather like a hybrid of structure and light. A few points of white in a view constellate and create their own journey, while white verticals are the most powerful of all as they jump out of the surrounding flowers and act like route markers.

Light and shade: I am drawn to scenes with dramatic contrast between light and shade when I am taking photographs. Arresting views often occur where the dark colours of yew and box extend the palette of greens beyond what seems feasible in the prevailing light, and this explains why they have such a dramatic impact around the garden. When photographing individual flowers, sunlight gives them an extra dimension because it adds tints and shades either side of the main flower colour via shadow, illumination, and reflection. This gives each flower its own little palette of colours that harmonize with each other, rather like turning a single note into a chord. Growing different flowers in a range of tints and shades of the same colour together would capture this effect on a larger scale, making the whole flowerbed seem to shimmer even on cloudy days.

Leaf colour: as I was creating the garden, I quickly learned the importance of variation in leaf colour for adding interest to the flowerbeds beyond their blooming seasons. Yet from the photographs it is clear there is another effect at work, particularly in larger spaces. Blue light scatters faster than other colours giving distant objects a blue tinge, and this is used by artists to create a sense of scale in landscape compositions. In the garden it tricks the brain into thinking areas of grey and blue-green foliage are further away than they really are. The effect is even more powerful on dull or misty days, and this illusion could be harnessed deliberately to help a design retreat into the distance. By the same mechanism, lime-coloured leaves and flowers appear closer, which explains their enlivening effect and why *Euphorbia* and *Alchemilla* seem to jump out from the surrounding plants.

Left: Towering yew sentries beside the rose garden arch help to trigger a sense of child-like wonder.

The twilight zone: I chose the blue, silver, and white colour scheme in the mirrored borders to reflect the sky above and to avoid causing localized points of focus by triggering our hardwired berry-gathering instincts. But by moving back and forth between the borders and the rose garden while taking photographs it has become clear that another effect is at work. As light levels fall, our vision switches to a combination of rods and cones and only these colours are still perceptible. I have accidentally enhanced the dreamy restfulness of the borders by suggesting to the brain the possibility that the light is fading, as in any natural environment the only way to see just these colours would be at twilight.

Horizontal lines: I wasn't aware of how limiting horizontal lines are until I started taking photographs and realized they bring the visual journey to an abrupt halt. They seem to act as artificial horizons and tell the brain that whatever led up to them stops here, so don't bother thinking beyond this point. Even photographs showing a small horizontal section of the top of a wall shut down the imagination. The same wall viewed from an oblique angle transforms it into a diagonal line full of perspective, possibility, and freedom, so it isn't the wall that is the problem, but rather anything that appears as a level horizon across the field of view.

Height, scale, and framing: moving the camera up or down changes the emotional impact of an image of the same scene, and this is because we experience a space as it relates to our own physical form. If there is too much height, the space feels imposing and inaccessible; too little and we feel like giants in our own land. Indeed, it was the camera angle that generated the sense of immersion I remember from childhood photographs and that I set out to replicate in my own rose garden. Capturing these effects deliberately on the ground is a powerful way to steer the emotional impact of a garden's design. Framing is another element in the composition of photographs that would translate well into a garden setting, and adding something that arches overhead or flanks an existing feature could transform an uninspiring view.

Breaking the spell: when there is something in the field of view that looks as if it doesn't belong there, filtering it out uses considerable mental energy and interferes with our ability to experience the scene in an open and unguarded way. When everything you see is intentionally part of the composition, however, focus can be diffuse and meandering and there is no need to maintain mental discipline to edit anything out. This reinforces the importance of embracing existing features and thoughtfully embedding them into the garden's design wherever possible.

Structure and layout in winter: taking weekly photographs throughout the winter is fascinating as it has motivated me to really study the garden when it is looking its worst. When there is nothing left but permanent layout and structure, their impact in defining the view is laid bare. In the garden here the two extremes are the mirrored borders where structure is dominant and unyielding, and parts of the pastels garden where it is virtually non-existent. In winter the mirrored borders hold onto their identity just as strongly as in summer, but the pastels garden loses its character and turns into a scruffy field.

FINDING YOUR OWN STYLE

I took the decision not to visit other gardens and instead to restrict myself to primary sources of inspiration such as natural landscapes and wild plants when designing the garden here. My aim was to keep my mental drawing board pristine and free from human influence as much as possible, while opening it up to everything Mother Nature has to offer. Rather than being the product of current fashion or a prevailing school of thought, as a result my garden has a distinctive otherworldly feel quite unlike anywhere else. In the same way I am sure that everyone has their own unique style hidden away, and I hope the steps below will help you to find yours.

> Truly original ideas well up from within, but inner vision is fragile.

Keep your creative palette clean: truly original ideas well up from within, but inner vision is fragile and easily blotted out by images from the outside world, so to avoid creating a patchwork of other people's ideas, insulate your imagination to protect your creative palette. Only when you have settled on your original design theme is it safe to reach out and compile a list of suitable components such as plants, hard landscaping materials, and garden furniture. Then, withdraw your attention from the outer world back into your imagination to work out how to use the components to create a real-world version of your inner vision. This is a very rewarding process and the end result will be entirely your own.

Study your reactions: we tend to take it at face value when something appeals to us, but by really studying what is behind your preferences you will be able to extract patterns and common features that are a guide to what will contribute best to your own style. It may be that unusual textures appeal to you, or perhaps you are drawn to intricacy, spirals, or rich dark colours. By closely analysing your reactions, you can create a personalized profile to inform your design choices.

Be bold: if you have put the time and effort into coming up with a style that is original, uncompromising, and based around elements that appeal to you, have the courage to really go for it. It is tempting to dabble with a new design theme to test the water and see how it looks, but something I have learned here is that committing with both feet gives your ideas the best chance of success. In many ways a garden is like a stage or film set, and complete immersion is the only way to find out what it will feel like to be in a world of your own making.

Don't compromise with an imagined audience: your garden is just that – yours. Other people will have their own tastes and opinions about how a garden should look, and that is what their own gardens are for. The pressure to conform is so often about dominance rather than the right or wrong way to do something, and you will be amazed by how quickly people get behind you if you summon the confidence to plough on and do your own thing. Who knows, they may even end up copying you.

Overleaf: With the herbaceous plants felled for winter, the contribution of the layout and structural elements to the mirrored borders is plain to see.

I developed a range of design methods and techniques while working out how to turn my ideas and observations into a garden on the ground, and this chapter shares some of them in the hope that they will be useful to other gardeners.

Chapter Six

DESIGN TECHNIQUES

Left: Iris *'Winter Olympics'* and white foxgloves in the mirrored borders show how variation in flower size, texture, and form come to the fore within a restricted colour scheme.

DESIGN TECHNIQUES

SUCCESSIONAL BLOOMING IN FIXED ROLES

Right: By the end of September, wands of Sanguisorba tenuifolia var. alba *and banks of powder-blue asters turn the borders into a pair of breaking waves.*

As areas of the garden became established, one thing I noticed was the highly seasonal nature of the displays, so when I was designing the mirrored borders I wanted to find a way to smooth them into a more continuous show right across the growing season, while still allowing the plants to set seed for the benefit of wildlife. Inspired by the way similar-looking wildflowers often follow each other into bloom, I developed a form of successional planting using perennials that contribute a similar colour and texture but flower at different times of year, so that they could take over fixed roles from each other. As it was experimental, this idea was only one of the considerations I used when drawing up the design, but it worked so well that it could be applied much more intensively in a new planting scheme, or used to decide what to add to an existing one.

The technique consists of creating a design based on plant roles instead of plant varieties and then using a changing cast of plants to fill these roles through the growing season. As long as they are similarly spaced and in places that have the same degree of impact, the plants that perform these roles do not necessarily need to be next to each other, and the way they are laid out in the mirrored borders has the effect of recreating the same view but with a slightly different texture and balance over time.

> The technique consists of creating a design based on plant roles instead of plant varieties.

The illustrations that follow give you an idea of how it works and the plants are laid out on a flowering timeline to show roughly when they bloom here, with those also featured in Chapter Four marked with an asterisk*. The examples I have used are listed in the order they bloom, and they all grow in my garden so they were chosen to suit my conditions. I am sure that with a little time and some internet searches, options could be found in a range of flower colours and textures to suit most growing conditions.

WHITE SPIRES

1. ***Camassia leichtlinii* 'Alba'***: camassias are a valuable source of late spring colour, and they work well en masse and in small groups dotted through neighbouring perennial clumps.
2. **Lupin, white varieties:** lupins form bushy plants with very attractive leaves, and the flowers are dense pillars of colour that are visible over long distances.
3. ***Digitalis purpurea* f. *albiflora****: white foxgloves are a remarkable sight in early summer, when they soar up through the surrounding plants like rods of pure light. They resonate with each other over very large distances, so work well spread throughout the garden in ones and twos.
4. ***Delphinium elatum*, white varieties:** delphiniums are large and eye-catching plants with plush columns of colour that can reach considerable height. They look best grown in small groups at key points along lines of sight.
5. ***Aconitum napellus* subsp. *vulgare* 'Albidum'**: this lovely monkshood looks very like an understated delphinium, and as it comes into bloom just as the delphiniums fade, it is ideal for taking over their role.
6. ***Verbascum chaixii* 'Album'***: an elegant and versatile plant that is ideally placed to take over the role performed by foxgloves. Its slender rods of small white flowers have the most impact piercing through surrounding plants in ones and twos.
7. ***Epilobium* (*Chamaenerion*) *angustifolium* 'Album'***: white rosebay willowherb is also a superb source of tall white spires after the foxgloves, although it tends to form large localized colonies so is best placed where a dense block of stems is required.
8. ***Veronicastrum virginicum* 'Album'**: this slender and ethereal plant is a last echo of summer, and it stands apart from the late season mayhem with pristine spires that work equally well in large groups or as solitary accents.

DESIGN TECHNIQUES

MAY

JUNE

JULY

AUGUST

SEPTEMBER

PINK CLOUDS

1. ***Phuopsis stylosa****: growing as a low spreading carpet of mossy leaves, this charming plant harmlessly weaves through its neighbours and is covered with fluffy pink pompoms right through the peak rose season.
2. ***Thalictrum aquilegiifolium,* pink varieties**: this early-flowering meadow rue is a good source of colour at height, and it works well dotted through late spring bulbs where its fluffy flowers and slender frame are a wonderful contrast. It needs reliably moist soil and at least part shade, so it is perfect for a gloomy corner.
3. ***Astilbe,* pink varieties**: astilbes form neat mounds of attractive leaves below feathery plumes of tiny flowers. They are ideal to take over from *Thalictrum aquilegiifolium* as they also prefer a moist, shady spot.
4. ***Sanguisorba obtusa***: a charming plant that grows as a slowly spreading mat of dense, woody roots with attractive, scented leaves. With its wands of fluffy pink catkin flowers, it is well placed to take over from *Phuopsis stylosa*.
5. ***Filipendula rubra***: this enchanting meadowsweet grows as a spreading colony of woody roots with a sparse carpet of palmate leaves. The candyfloss flowers are held at head height on very strong slender stems. It looks best grown en masse rather than in small clumps and is well placed to take over from *Thalictrum aquilegiifolium* as it is very similar in structure.
6. ***Eupatorium cannabinum***: wild hemp agrimony is a robust plant that grows as a dense block of leafy stems topped with fluffy, domed flowerheads. It is ideal where a mass of soft pink clouds is needed as a backdrop.
7. ***Persicaria campanulata***: a valuable source of late-season colour, this knotweed spreads to form a large dense thicket of flowering stems covered in tiny heather-like bells in late summer.
8. ***Saponaria officinalis****: a leafy carpeting plant that grows well alongside *Phuopsis stylosa*, and is a very good source of soft pink ground cover towards the end of summer.
9. ***Symphyotrichum ericoides* 'Pink Cloud'**: a pink form of white heath aster that could step into a role left vacant by *Astilbe* and provide end-of-season softness with fluffy sprays of tiny pink flowers in autumn.

DESIGN TECHNIQUES

MAY

JUNE

JULY

AUGUST

SEPTEMBER
& OCTOBER

159

BLUE SPIRES

1. *Veronica gentianoides*: this lovely little plant grows as a small leafy mat and bears slender spires of pale blue speedwell flowers in late spring.
2. *Camassia leichtlinii* **subsp.** *suksdorfii* **Caerulea Group**: a powder-blue camassia that flowers in late spring and is happy to grow in small groups between neighbouring perennial clumps.
3. **Lupin, blue varieties**: lupins are available in a rainbow of colours, making them a very useful source of dense blue spires in late spring and early summer.
4. *Delphinium elatum,* **blue varieties**: blue delphiniums have proved to be the healthiest and longest lived in the garden here. They are breathtaking in full bloom and a very hard act to follow.
5. *Veronica longifolia*: this plant is most effective grown en masse so the slender spires of tiny flowers can add a brushstroke-like texture to the view.
6. *Aconitum napellus*: this lovely monkshood is similar in structure and habit to a delphinium but with a slighter build. It comes into bloom just in time to step into the vacant role of tall blue spires and it delivers admirably, particularly when grown in small groups.
7. *Veronicastrum virginicum,* **blue varieties**: a superb source of texture when planted en masse, each mature plant produces up to 20 tall leafy stems topped with very slender, pointed spires of tiny flowers.
8. *Aconitum carmichaelii* **'Arendsii'**: this richly coloured, autumn-flowering monkshood provides a last echo of the blue spires of summer.

DESIGN TECHNIQUES

MAY

JUNE

JULY

AUGUST

SEPTEMBER

161

VIOLET HAZE

1. ***Thalictrum aquilegiifolium***: this species of meadow rue flowers in pink, pale violet, and white, making it an excellent early-season source of colour at height.
2. ***Knautia arvensis*** *****: a local wildflower that graces the verges with a haze of soft-lavender buttons in early summer, field scabious makes a superb garden plant that works well interspersed with other airy perennials.
3. ***Thalictrum rochebruneanum*** *****: this elegant meadow rue reaches a considerable height quite early in the season, and the panicles of tiny pendent flowers are followed by attractive burgundy seedheads. It needs a moist, partly shady spot and looks best growing in small groups, making it ideal for taking up the role vacated by *Thalictrum aquilegiifolium*.
4. ***Allium cristophii*** *****: this magical allium is fascinating viewed close up, but really comes into its own planted en masse when the flowerheads merge into a shimmering haze of metallic violet stars. Ideal for growing between later-flowering perennials that will hide the allium's straggly leaves during the flowering season.
5. ***Salvia verticillata*** *****: a low sprawling salvia similar in habit to *Knautia arvensis* that flowers in high summer over a long period with tiny trumpet flowers from long-lasting, violet-flushed bracts. It is a very good filler plant with a gift for stitching neighbouring perennials together.
6. ***Limonium platyphyllum*** *****: an enchanting little plant that produces very densely branching heads of slim wiry stems covered in tiny pale violet flowers that merge into a soft mist en masse. It works well grown at repeating intervals between plants with stronger outlines, and is ideal for taking over a role from *Allium cristophii*.
7. ***Thalictrum delavayi***: this lovely late-flowering meadow rue has delicate maidenhair-fern-like leaves and tall slender flowering stems bearing masses of tiny, anemone-like flowers in a beautiful shade of lilac. It looks best weaving in between more substantial neighbours and is perfect for taking over from *Thalictrum rochebruneanum*.
8. ***Succisa pratensis,* mauve seedlings** *****: a locally common wildflower indispensable in the garden for late-season colour that sits as a neat leafy clump right through the summer and then produces a haze of violet bobbles on slender, wiry stems. It is very similar in habit to *Knautia arvensis* and they choose to grow together here, making them a natural choice for the same role.
9. ***Verbena bonariensis***: this tall, airy plant has branching, angular stems topped with small clouds of violet flowers. It has a variable flowering season, but makes its greatest contribution in late summer and early autumn.

DESIGN TECHNIQUES

MAY

JUNE

JULY

AUGUST

SEPTEMBER
& OCTOBER

WHITE FOAM

1. *Allium cowanii (A. neapolitanum* **Cowanii Group***)*: a small lax-stemmed allium with loose balls of pure white flowers that spreads into large colonies where the flowers merge together like seafoam. It is ideal for lining a path where the flowers can loll to their best effect.
2. *Allium nigrum*: a strongly upright allium with subtly shaded white and green flowers that looks superb stretching away into the distance, this early summer-flowering bulb is well placed to step into the shoes of *Allium cowanii*.
3. *Centranthus ruber* **'Albus'***: the delicate feathery plumes of this naturalized wildflower disguise a tough and drought-proof character, making it ideal for hot dry sites and cracks in walls and patios. It also grows happily in a sunny flowerbed and looks very effective weaving through more substantial neighbours.
4. *Valeriana officinalis**: an extremely elegant plant producing tall airy stems from a small leafy base that branch into soft white clouds of tiny lily-scented flowers. It is ideal for filling the role left vacant by *Centranthus ruber* 'Albus'.
5. *Filipendula ulmaria*: wild meadowsweet prefers a moist, shady spot where it will spread to form a colony of strongly upright stems topped with fluffy, ivory flowers.
6. *Phlox paniculata,* **white varieties**: grown en masse, the fluttering flowerheads of phlox merge into a meandering swathe of white that is very effective when viewed from a distance.
7. *Sanguisorba tenuifolia* **var.** *alba**: a very dramatic plant with tall, slender wands bearing swarms of pendent, white catkin flowers that sway in the wind like sea spray. This beautiful *Sanguisorba* brings back the foamy softness of *Valeriana officinalis* right at the end of summer.
8. *Sedum (Hylotelephium) spectabile,* **white varieties**: pure white sedum flowerheads take on the look of a snowdrift when they crowd together, and grown en masse they end the season with a charming echo of the foaming waves of *Allium cowanii* back in spring.

DESIGN TECHNIQUES

MAY

JUNE

JULY

AUGUST

SEPTEMBER

BLUE BILLOWS

1. ***Nepeta* x *faassenii***: a sprawling mound of grey-green leafy stems bearing pretty blue trumpet flowers, catmint is a valuable source of colour and texture that is most effective grown in groups and beside a path or patio.
2. ***Amsonia tabernaemontana* var. *salicifolia***: a very polite plant that slowly spreads to form a small colony of slender upright stems bearing clusters of steely-blue flowers.
3. ***Eryngium bourgatii****: a low, mound-forming plant that produces numerous flowering stems above silver-veined leaves, this sea holly looks best grown in large groups where its texture makes a real impact between softer neighbours.
4. ***Campanula lactiflora****: this enormous plant dominates the garden here in July when its tall billowing stems are weighed down with hundreds of soft blue bells. It is very effective grown en masse and viewed from a distance as it creates a large block of colour, but it also works well dotted through shrubs and other tall perennials.
5. ***Perovskia atriplicifolia* (*Salvia*) 'Blue Spire'**: a small woody-framed shrub that echoes the blue billows of earlier *Campanula lactiflora* in the mirrored borders. A few plants grown together create a block of feathery blue in a long view, while individual plants are an eye-catching contrast to leafy planting.
6. ***Catananche caerulea***: elegant and slender framed, this plant is very well suited to the edge of paths and patios where its billowing stems of papery cornflowers can sprawl to best effect.
7. ***Aster* x *frikartii* 'Wunder von Stäfa'**: this beautiful aster grows as a sprawling mound of leafy stems and bears large daisy flowers over an extraordinarily long period, making it a very useful low-growing source of late-season blue.
8. ***Symphyotrichum* 'Little Carlow'**: a reliable Michaelmas daisy that steps into the role of blue billows in the mirrored borders in September, where in combination with *Sanguisorba* and white *Sedum*, it performs the final act of the season.

DESIGN TECHNIQUES

JUNE

JULY

AUGUST

SEPTEMBER

OCTOBER

167

DESIGN TECHNIQUES

RESTRICTED COLOUR SCHEMES

Left: In late May the rose garden is dominated by shades of purple, mauve, and pink.

Quite early in the process of designing the garden, I realized that using more than three main colours in an area would make it look busy and incoherent. I had already noticed that the most visually appealing wildflower communities and landscape views in the countryside were always in a restricted range of colours. As a result, all areas of the garden here are carefully colour schemed, and this makes a very strong contribution to the overall character of the place. Below are some of the benefits gleaned from my experience of designing and gardening with restricted colour schemes.

They are flexible and accommodating: as a technique for creating effective planting, a restricted colour scheme is surprisingly easy to work with. The beds will look thoughtful and visually coherent with almost any combination of plants, as long as you stick to your chosen colours. In effect the colour scheme itself does the heavy lifting, leaving you free to play around and explore different plant options and combinations without compromising the overall visual impact of the garden.

They establish mood: colour is a powerful trigger for emotion, making it a very useful tool for evoking a particular mood or feeling. Choosing roses in a sugar-sweet colour palette contributes to the sense of abundance in my rose garden, and the romantic qualities of the space are in large part due to restricting the perennial flower colours to harmonious shades of pink, mauve, and blue highlighted with silver, white, and the lime colours of *Euphorbia* and *Alchemilla*. In stark contrast, the tranquillity of the mirrored borders is entirely due to the colour scheme, as the shades of blue, silver, and white reflect the sky above and merge into a continuous landscape without the localized distraction of anything that would trigger gathering instincts by looking edible.

They indicate thought and planning: on first impressions the truly feral nature of much of my garden is obscured, and this is mostly due to the colour schemes. This visual evidence of restriction and restraint is an instant and powerful way to show the reassuring presence of a human hand.

They help to avoid unintended colour clashes: once a colour scheme has been decided, all sorts of design risks just melt away, such as unintended colour clashes along lines of sight. Blobs of the wrong colour in peripheral vision or in the distance can have a surprisingly strong impact on how well a planting scheme works by breaking the spell or drawing in its horizons, but with an overarching colour scheme in place everything will always gel together.

They are highly compatible with an ornamental ecosystem: another reason I chose a restricted colour scheme in the rose garden was that I needed the herbaceous perennials to work well in any combination. They were destined to self-sow anywhere they chose in the rose-garden beds, so it was very important that wherever they popped up they would look at home. It would have been almost impossible to allow the plants so much freedom without sacrificing visual harmony and coherence if I had used a wider range of colours.

They create relatedness across large areas: a small garden can be very effective with a wide range of colours to increase variety and interest at close quarters, but larger spaces really benefit from techniques to create relatedness to give them a single unified identity. A restricted colour scheme combined with repeating structural motifs is a simple and effective way to achieve this.

They encourage more adventurous plant choices: having to find plants that fit within a colour scheme casts a different light on the selection process. It encourages you to explore and aim for the widest-possible range of plants within your chosen colours rather than just growing things that are already familiar or widely available.

They can differentiate garden rooms: when working with garden rooms, it is tempting to use a range of styles to give them individual character, but differentiating the areas from each other stylistically can detract from the identity and character of the garden as a whole. Rather than mimic a range of garden styles, using different colour schemes can instead give each area a distinct feel while still allowing your own style to shine through across the board.

They throw focus onto other aspects of the plants and the design: usually the first thing we notice about a flower is its colour, but within a restricted colour scheme flower colour becomes much less of a draw and focus is instead redirected onto more subtle characteristics of the plants. I used this effect deliberately in the design of the mirrored borders where variation in leaf shape and colour, and in flower size, texture, and form were emphasized in order to create interest within the very restricted range of flower colours. In a similar way, a restricted colour scheme also throws elements of the layout and design into the spotlight, as they do not retreat into the background under a cacophony of colours.

SAMPLE COLOUR SCHEMES
New design concepts and colour schemes continued to crystallize in my mind long after I had finished creating my own, and with no space left to fill on the ground, I stored them as image montages and plant lists instead. I am very happy to share some of these on the following pages, together with a montage and plants list for the mirrored borders, in the hope that they will provide a useful starting point for other gardeners interested in exploring this technique at home.

Focusing on the colour scheme requires a greater degree of precision over plant choices, so the plants listed overleaf include some named varieties alongside the perennial species, which are shown with just a botanical name. I have also included hard landscaping materials because the colours, shapes, and textures of walls and paths are an important part of the finished effect, and these will be a useful guide if you are choosing a restricted colour scheme to suit existing features.

The plant lists were drawn up with no particular site in mind, so the suggestions would need to be researched to check their suitability for your garden, and they are in no way exhaustive so please view them as a starting point from which to add your own choices. As long as plants chosen from the lists suit the environmental constraints of your plot, then they are fully compatible with my gardening methods, and the herbaceous species suggested are all potential candidates for a self-sowing perennial understorey.

DESIGN TECHNIQUES

MELLOW

A combination of pale-yellow and purple flowers with lots of silver and verdigris foliage, this colour scheme would create a mellow and welcoming feel and work very well on a larger scale or surrounding a house or patio. Plants to consider:

Bulbs
Allium giganteum (2)
Allium hollandicum 'Purple Sensation'
Crocus tommasinianus

Herbaceous plants
Achillea 'Credo'
Aconitum lycoctonum subsp. *vulparia*
Alchemilla mollis (3)
Angelica archangelica (biennial)
Aquilegia chrysantha
Artemisia absinthium 'Lambrook Mist'
Artemisia ludoviciana 'Silver Queen'
Artemisia 'Powis Castle'
Cephalaria gigantea (1)
Corydalis lutea
Cynara cardunculus (7)
Digitalis lutea
Eryngium agavifolium
Eryngium eburneum
Eryngium giganteum (biennial)
Eryngium leavenworthii
Foeniculum vulgare (9)

Helleborus argutifolius
Iris 'Lemon Ice' (14)
Iris 'Sable' (4)
Kniphofia 'Little Maid'
Liatris spicata 'Floristan Violett'
Limonium platyphyllum (10)
Linaria purpurea
Linaria vulgaris
Macleaya cordata (x *kewensis*)
Melica altissima 'Atropurpurea'
Nepeta govaniana
Onopordum acanthium (biennial)
Phlomis russeliana (11)
Salvia verticillata
Sisyrinchium striatum
Succisa pratensis (8)
Thalictrum 'Elin'
Thalictrum delavayi (5)
Thalictrum flavum subsp. *glaucum*
Thalictrum rochebruneanum
Verbascum chaixii
Verbascum (Cotswold Group) 'Gainsborough'
Verbascum thapsus (biennial) (12)

Verbena bonariensis
Veronicastrum virginicum 'Fascination' (13)

Climbers
Clematis 'Jackmanii'
Clematis 'Polish Spirit'
Wisteria, purple varieties

Shrubs and trees
Buddleja 'Nanho Purple'
Buddleja alternifolia
Corylus avellana
Euphorbia characias subsp. *wulfenii*
Helichrysum italicum
Lavandula stoechas
Phygelius aequalis 'Yellow Trumpet'
Ruta graveolens (6)
Santolina pinnata subsp. *neapolitana* 'Edward Bowles'
Syringa vulgaris 'Katherine Havemeyer'

TRANQUIL

This is the colour scheme I used in the mirrored borders with flowers in shades of blue and white and a focus on silvery stem and leaf colours. Together they mimic the sky in all its moods and create a tranquil and contemplative space. This colour scheme would work well in a small, airy garden, but it really comes into its own under a large expanse of sky. Plants to consider:

Bulbs
Allium cowanii (*A. neapolitanum* Cowanii Group)
Allium nigrum
Tulipa 'Spring Green'
Tulipa 'White Triumphator'

Herbaceous plants
Aconitum x *bicolor*
Aconitum napellus
Agapanthus, Headbourne hybrids
Anemone x *hybrida* 'Honorine Jobert' (1)
Aquilegia vulgaris, blues and whites
Artemisia ludoviciana 'Silver Queen' (2)
Aster x *frikartii* 'Wunder von Stäfa' (4)
Campanula lactiflora (9)
Crambe maritima
Cynara cardunculus (8)
Delphinium, dark blue varieties
Delphinium, mid-blue varieties
Delphinium, white varieties
Digitalis purpurea f. *albiflora* (biennial)
Echinops exaltatus (5)
Echinops ritro
Eryngium bourgatii (11)
Eryngium eburneum
Iris 'Black Swan'
Iris 'Braithwaite'
Iris 'Jane Phillips'
Iris 'White City' (13)
Leucanthemum x *superbum*
Liatris spicata 'Alba'
Macleaya cordata (x *kewensis*)
Onopordum acanthium (biennial)
Phlox paniculata 'Mount Fuji' (6)
Salvia nemorosa
Salvia x *sylvestris* 'Mainacht'
Sanguisorba tenuifolia var. *alba* (12)
Sedum spectabile 'Iceberg' (10)
Succisa pratensis
Symphyotrichum 'Little Carlow' (3)
Verbascum chaixii 'Album'
Veronicastrum virginicum 'Album'
Veronicastrum virginicum, blue (14)

Climbers
Clematis 'Blue Angel' (7)
Clematis 'Perle d'Azur'
Clematis 'Polish Spirit'
Wisteria sinensis

Shrubs and trees
Buxus sempervirens
Euphorbia characias subsp. *wulfenii*
Hydrangea arborescens 'Annabelle'
Magnolia stellata
Perovskia 'Blue Spire'
Romneya coulteri
Rosa x *alba* 'Alba Maxima'
Rosa 'Snowdon'
Syringa vulgaris 'Madame Lemoine'
Taxus baccata 'Fastigiata'
Viburnum opulus 'Roseum'

DESIGN TECHNIQUES

REFRESHING

A simple refreshing colour scheme that is ideal for a wilder space and well suited to an area with light shade from existing trees. It captures the feel of an open woodland in late spring, but with successional planting anchored by the white trunks of Himalayan birch, it could be persuaded to hold onto that freshness throughout the summer. Plants to consider:

Bulbs
Allium nigrum
Eranthis hyemalis
Erythronium 'Pagoda'
Erythronium californicum 'White Beauty'
Hyacinthoides non-scripta 'Alba' (11)
Ornithogalum nutans
Tulipa 'Spring Green'
Tulipa 'White Triumphator'

Herbaceous plants
Aconitum lycoctonum subsp. *vulparia*
Alchemilla conjuncta
Alchemilla mollis
Anemone nemorosa (1)
Angelica archangelica (biennial)
Anthriscus sylvestris (biennial) (2)
Asplenium scolopendrium (3)
Campanula alliariifolia (4)
Campanula lactiflora 'Alba'
Chasmanthium latifolium
Convallaria majalis
Digitalis grandiflora (8)
Digitalis lutea
Digitalis purpurea f. *albiflora* (biennial) (7)
Epilobium angustifolium 'Album' (9)
Epimedium x *youngianum* 'Niveum'
Euphorbia amygdaloides var. *robbiae* (10)
Euphorbia polychroma
Filipendula hexapetala
Filipendula ulmaria
Galium mollugo
Galium odoratum
Galium sylvaticum
Galium verum
Hesperis matronalis var. *albiflora* (biennial)
Lamprocapnos spectabilis 'Alba' (6)
Lunaria annua var. *albiflora* (biennial)
Luzula nivea
Matteuccia struthiopteris (13)
Oxalis acetosella
Paris quadrifolia
Polygonatum x *hybridum*
Primula veris
Primula vulgaris (14)
Silene vulgaris
Tellima grandiflora
Teucrium scorodonia (15)
Trillium grandiflorum (16)
Veratum album

Climbers
Humulus lupulus (12)
Lonicera periclymenum

Shrubs and trees
Betula utilis subsp. *jacquemontii*
Corylopsis pauciflora
Corylus avellana (5)
Hamamelis x *intermedia* 'Pallida'
Philadelphus 'Virginal'
Ribes nigrum
Ribes sanguineum 'White Icicle'
Ribes uva-crispa
Rosa x *alba* 'Alba Semiplena'
Sambucus nigra
Viburnum opulus

NOSTALGIC

A delicate colour scheme that captures the simplicity of childhood with wiry and papery-textured plants and naturalistic flower forms in pastel shades of blue, mauve, and pink. It is inspired by childhood memories of looking for wildflowers by the beach, and is well suited to flint and shingle hard landscaping and sun-bleached wood. This colour scheme would work on any scale and is ideal for a windswept hilltop or coastal location with far-reaching views. Plants to consider:

Bulbs
Narcissus 'Thalia'
Puschkinia libanotica
Scilla siberica 'Alba'

Herbaceous plants
Achillea 'Appleblossom' (1)
Agapanthus 'Sea Coral'
Althaea officinalis (2)
Anaphalis triplinervis (3)
Anemone tomentosa
Aquilegia vulgaris, pale pink
Armeria maritima 'Alba'
Artemisia absinthium 'Lambrook Mist'
Artemisia ludoviciana 'Silver Queen' (4)
Artemisia schmidtiana 'Nana'
Astrantia maxima
Campanula alliariifolia
Campanula lactiflora 'Loddon Anna'
Campanula persicifolia 'Chettle Charm'
Cardamine pratensis
Catananche caerulea (5)
Centaurea montana 'Alba'
Centranthus ruber 'Albus'
Crambe maritima
Cynara cardunculus
Dipsacus fullonum (biennial) (6)
Echinops ritro (7)
Echinops sphaerocephalus
Erigeron 'Quakeress'
Eryngium eburneum
Eryngium giganteum (biennial) (8)
Eryngium maritimum
Eryngium variifolium (9)
Filipendula rubra
Filipendula ulmaria
Gaura 'The Bride'
Geranium pratense 'Silver Queen'
Geranium sanguineum var. *striatum*
Iris 'Blue Shimmer'
Iris 'White City'
Knautia arvensis (10)
Monarda fistulosa
Morina longifolia
Salvia sclarea var. *turkestanica* (biennial) (13)
Salvia verticillata 'Alba'
Scabiosa 'Pink Mist'
Sedum spectabile 'Iceberg'
Silene uniflora
Stachys byzantina (14)
Stokesia laevis 'Träumeri' (15)
Valeriana officinalis
Veronicastrum virginicum 'Album' (16)
Veronicastrum virginicum f. *roseum*

Climbers
Clematis 'Little Nell'
Clematis 'Maria Cornelia'
Lathyrus latifolius 'Rosa Perle'
Passiflora caerulea (11)

Shrubs and trees
Balotta pseudodictamnus
Lavandula stoechas
Phlomis italica (12)
Pyrus salicifolia 'Pendula'
Rosmarinus officinalis
Salix exigua

BOUNTIFUL

A rich and heart-warming colour scheme that is well suited to a larger garden with mature trees, and as it harmonizes with brickwork it would be a very effective way to connect a red-brick house to a leafy horizon. It has a naturally autumnal feel so could be used as a companion to the springlike refreshing colour scheme. Plants to consider:

Bulbs
Narcissus bulbocodium subsp. *bulbocodium* var. *conspicuus*
Tulipa 'Amber Glow'
Tulipa 'National Velvet'

Herbaceous plants
Achillea 'Inca Gold' (1)
Achillea millefolium 'Red Velvet'
Alchemilla mollis
Angelica gigas (biennial)
Aquilegia vulgaris var. *stellata* 'Ruby Port' (2)
Asplenium scolopendrium
Astrantia 'Bloody Mary'
Astrantia 'Hadspen Blood' (4)
Calamagrostis x *acutiflora* 'Karl Foerster'
Centaurea macrocephala
Chasmanthium latifolium
Crocosmia x *crocosmiiflora* 'Honey Angels' (11)
Dicentra formosa 'Bacchanal'
Dierama pulcherrimum 'Blackbird'
Digitalis ferruginea (12)
Digitalis lanata
Echinacea 'Harvest Moon' (14)
Epimedium x *versicolor* 'Sulphureum'
Eupatorium purpureum
Euphorbia griffithii
Foeniculum vulgare (5)
Foeniculum vulgare 'Giant Bronze'
Geranium phaeum
Helenium hoopesii
Helenium 'Moerheim Beauty'
Helleborus argutifolius
Hemerocallis 'Corky' (3)
Hemerocallis 'Stafford' (13)
Inula magnifica (9)
Iris 'Action Front'
Iris 'Kent Pride' (8)
Iris 'Quechee'
Iris 'Rajah'
Melica altissima 'Atropurpurea'
Miscanthus sinensis 'Rotsilber'
Molinia caerulea subsp. *arundinacea*
Penstemon 'Garnet'
Rheum palmatum (10)
Rudbeckia fulgida var. *sullivantii* 'Goldsturm'
Sanguisorba officinalis (6)
Sanguisorba tenuifolia 'Purpurea'
Sedum 'Herbstfreude'
Solidago canadensis
Stipa gigantea (7)
Veratrum nigrum

Climbers
Clematis 'Royal Velours'
Clematis tangutica
Lonicera periclymenum

Shrubs and trees
Cotinus coggygria
Rosa 'Tuscany Superb'
Taxus baccata 'Fastigiata'

EXTENDING THE FLOWERING SEASON IN AN EXISTING GARDEN

I conceived of each area of the garden here as a fully formed place with plants represented by texture, colour, shape, and size long before I decided which real-life plants would be able to take on these roles. My approach has much to offer when attempting to improve an existing garden too, and I share below a step-by-step method first formulated for a local horticultural society. It combines this approach, my plant-choosing method, and the successional planting technique into a system for extending the flowering season in an existing garden.

Learning to observe

First of all, practise observing your environment in abstract terms rather than looking to identify the individual objects within it. This means deliberately focusing on the lines, angles, textures, colours, shapes, sizes, arrangements, and patterns that you are seeing. The goal is to become attuned to the sensory qualities of your surroundings and to get comfortable with wilfully ignoring the urge to know what things are. Practise observing things purely in these abstract terms until you can switch into this mode with ease. I did this while walking in the countryside, but your own garden seems the most sensible place to start.

Step one: observe your garden on all of its good days

Once you can scrutinize your surroundings without feeling the need to identify anything, the first step is to make a record of your garden's good days for a whole year. Again, focus only on the abstract – the shapes, colours, textures, and so on.

> The first step is to make a record of your garden's good days for a whole year.

Ignore your garden on its bad days: the motivation to make improvements might come from asking "What's wrong with the garden today?", but the solutions are going to be generated by asking "What's right with the garden today?", when it is looking its best. This record of your garden's good days will give you existing fixed points in a plan that will blend them into a more continuous sequence across time on the ground. The table on page 186 illustrates this using a simple example, but you can put as much detail into it as you like and even repeat the process year after year to monitor and make adjustments to your garden over time.

DESIGN TECHNIQUES

Step two: turning the good days into a continuous sequence
The second step is to decide where and when you'd like to repeat your favourite effects. Make a "consider adding" column to your chart and work through it deciding where and when you'd like to see each effect reappear in your garden during the growing season. Your aim is to blend your highlight snapshots into a more continuous display across your garden and across time. Cross-check that your additions will work with your existing highlights list to avoid adding anything that might upset the good days, and double-check your new additions will work well with each other at their peak times of year. As a by-product of this process, anything that isn't pulling its weight will be nudged out of your garden to make way for your new additions. The table illustrates this using a simple example, but again you can work in as much detail as you like, depending on how much change you want to make on the ground.

Right: Aster x frikartii *'Wunder von Stäfa'* is smothered in soft blue flowers from late July all the way through to October.

DESIGN TECHNIQUES

DESIGN TECHNIQUES

Left: Catananche caerulea *provides a charming burst of blue in August.*

Stick to working with abstract characteristics rather than identities, and don't be tempted to think about which plant might perform each role or even if such a plant exists: this part of the process is akin to writing the script, but not casting the actors. Turning a blind eye to possible candidates you are familiar with helps you to edge closer to your ideal rather than choosing the best fit from the knowledge you already have. Reality will come back into the process in the next step, when all your artistic decisions have been made.

Step three: identifying the plants

When you have finished your "consider adding" column, you will have a detailed plan for what to add where to amplify and extend all your favourite effects in your garden without altering its character or compromising your personal taste, and all without needing to know the name of a single new plant. You have effectively been working with hypothetical plant descriptions instead of real plant names, and to convert one to the other we need a tool that can find the best fit for a string of descriptive terms: an internet search engine. A plant's name and its description are just like an equation, and you already have the description side. A search engine will provide the name side for you by finding plants that match your description.

I use Google's image search out of habit, but no doubt other search engines would be equally effective. Type in your hypothetical plant's description as the search term, such as "vine with tiny white flowers in June", and Google's image search will show photographs of all the plants it can find that are described as such. A click on the image of a promising candidate usually reveals the plant's name, and then you can research its suitability for your site in the usual way before adding each choice to your chart.

If you can't find anything suitable from the search results, then get into the shoes of a person who might post the image onto the internet and rephrase your search terms accordingly, or try adjusting your criteria slightly. There is a knack to this, so experiment to find out what works best for you. Occasionally you will need to accept defeat and cross a hypothetical plant off your list, but you will be doing this from an informed position. If an option suitable for your site was accessible you would have found it. Go back to your "consider adding" column to see what other hypothetical plant would work, then hunt down a real one for that description instead. The completed table shows plant choices selected in this way.

185

DESIGN TECHNIQUES

Working through your list choosing plants for each role is a lovely way to spend the winter evenings. When the process is complete, you will have travelled full circle from observations on the ground, through the abstract, on to the hypothetical, into the actual and then back out onto the ground again. As a result of this process, you will have a plant-hunting list based on your personal taste and your existing garden, and that is full of unfamiliar but carefully considered and fully researched choices.

Right: Geranium pratense *and* Nepeta x faasennii *burst into bloom in early summer, just in time for the old rose season.*

Step 1 example Already got and love:	Step 2 example Consider adding:	Step 3 example Suitable plants for the role:
Low pink mound in June on the left of the front path	Low pink mound in September on the right of the front path	*Sedum* (**Hylotelephium**) *cauticola*
Tall blue spikes in July by the beech hedge	Tall blue spikes in September by the privet hedge	*Aconitum carmichaelii* 'Arendsii'
White sprays over the shed in July	White sprays over the garage in May and June	*Hydrangea petiolaris*
Tall blue billows in June and July to the right of the lawn	Tall blue billows in September or October to the left of the lawn	*Symphyotrichum* 'Little Carlow'
Sprawling white foam under the arbour in June	Sprawling white foam in front of the arbour in August	*Agapanthus* 'Headbourne White'

There is a big difference between harnessing natural systems to achieve a goal and giving up control to them, and it is only with discipline and forethought that their benefits can be incorporated into the garden. In this chapter I share some of what is necessary behind the scenes to stay in control while living and gardening so close to the wild.

Chapter Seven

STAYING IN CONTROL

Left: As the rose garden surges into growth in late April, my annual cycle of jobs ensures the garden is shipshape at the start of the growing season.

STAYING IN CONTROL

MY GARDENING YEAR

Right: During the winter months Irish yew and box balls dominate the view in the mirrored borders.

My gardening philosophy determined the character and maintenance needs of the garden, and combined with a self-imposed constraint of five hours gardening time a day, this provided fertile ground for inventing ways to deliver what the garden and I need to thrive, resulting in a cycle of jobs through the year and methods for carrying out each task. Maintenance methods must respect the integrity of the ornamental ecosystem so anything that can't survive unaided is allowed to die, there is no deadheading, no fertilizing, no removing or adding of organic matter, no chemical treatment of pests and diseases, no disturbing mingled plant communities, and outside of the mirrored borders there is no removing of self-sown seedlings except to allow access. I am therefore restricted to thorough weeding, regular hoeing in the mirrored borders, mowing the lawns, chopping down the herbaceous stems in autumn, and raking over the soil surface before spring. The only high-maintenance elements of the garden are those that visually embody discipline in the form of the carefully trained roses, clipped yew hedges, and box topiary.

Moving a job by a few weeks can make all the difference to how much time it takes.

I have been gardening here for over 20 years so the schedule of jobs is well worked out, but I am always on the lookout for improvements, and with the impact of climate change becoming more apparent through earlier springs, warmer autumns, and summer heatwaves, there is advantage to be found in reassessing the timing of jobs. Moving a job by a few weeks can make all the difference to how much time it takes, how effective it is, and how enjoyable it is to do.

I think of the garden as a living work of art during the growing season so aesthetic considerations are paramount, but from November until the end of March it is a work zone with a completely different set of rules focused on efficiency and preparation. Let us start when the real work begins: with the autumn clear-up in November.

MY ANNUAL CYCLE OF JOBS

I devote the whole of November to strimming down the herbaceous plants with my trimmer mower. It is very similar to a walk-behind lawnmower but instead of a blade it has a strimmer cord. I set the cord to 10 centimetres (4 inches) above the ground and drive the machine over all the flowerbeds, going around anything that blooms on the previous year's stems. The first pass fells the old dead stems, and then I drive the machine over the beds a second time to chop the fallen stems into small pieces. These stay where they fall as a mulch that rots down into the soil over the winter.

I was inspired to use this method by watching forestry workers in the nearby woods clearing the top growth off the firebreaks in a similar way using a brush cutter, creating habitat for a diverse and thriving community of wildflowers in the process. It is a highly effective way for one person to clear a large area before the winter weather sets in, and it makes it possible for me to manage the garden by myself: to do the job by hand would literally take months. By the end of November, the beds are neat and tidy with only the shrubs and trees standing proud. The chopped-up plant matter creates a dense mat underfoot when pruning the roses in December, returns all the organic matter to the soil, and saves me from carting it all off to a compost heap and then dragging it all back again. It is very important that I make sure there are no weeds in the beds before I run the strimmer over them, as the method is designed to spread seeds far and wide so I need to be sure I'm not adding weed seeds to the mix. Dense woody material that would take too long to rot down is added to the permanent piles of sticks that are hidden around the garden for wildlife.

December is given over to pruning and training the roses and to shaping the larger evergreen shrubs. In the garden's early years I pruned and trained the roses in March, but spring heat prompted me to move the job to December. This gives them longer to adjust to their new positions and they have consistently produced more flowers the following summer as a result.

In January, February, and early March I work my way through the beds with a soil rake removing moss and any larger chunks of old stem, rooting out perennial weeds such as nettles and brambles, and carrying out any transplants planned during the previous growing season. This job would be best done in March, but given the size of the garden and frequent interruptions due to the weather, I need to make an early start to ensure I have enough time to get it all done before spring. It is a wonderful way to stay engaged with the garden during its dormant months and to make the few daylight hours really count towards the summer ahead. February is also the time to pressure-wash the rose-garden paths and the stone benches, which really lifts the overall look of the garden and sets the stage for the new growing season ahead.

By mid-March spring is in the air and a green haze is returning to the flowerbeds, the rose domes are covered in fresh new shoots, and everything is shipshape and ready for the spring surge. On 15th March every year I spend an afternoon planting tender vegetable seeds in the greenhouse. I settled on this date by trial and error and found it gives the seedlings long enough to grow into sturdy little plants by the time they are planted out two months later. The second half of March is a chance for spring-cleaning jobs, which include the annual painting of the obelisks in the mirrored borders and any other woodwork in need of attention. Very little is staked or supported here apart from the roses and the delphiniums. The other plants were chosen with the intention that they would splay and sprawl into each other, but there is nothing quite so forlorn as a collapsed rose or delphinium, so as the perennial crowns begin to shoot, the delphinium supports are placed back into position.

> By mid-March spring is in the air and a green haze is returning to the flowerbeds.

April begins with a flurry of activity in the nursery, as perennial crowns all around the garden are bristling with fresh shoots and this is the perfect time to lift some for propagating. Every year I pot up as many of the perennial species growing here as I can to make them available to visitors on the National Garden Scheme (NGS) open days through the summer. It is a joy to be able to pass on plants that have earned their spurs in my garden in the hope that they will not only be tough and healthy additions to visitors' plots, but may also go on to start little colonies of their own. The nursery is a popular feature on the open days and by the end of summer very little remains, so I spend the first week of April restocking it entirely. While I have been busy in the nursery and with spring cleaning, the weather has warmed up, the flowerbeds have surged into growth, and the garden has become a living work of art again. I spend the rest of April wandering through the beds with a glove and bucket removing any weeds and revelling in the beauty and energy of spring.

May, June, and July are an absolute joy, and despite the frenzy of activity in the beds there is very little for me to do but keep on top of the weeds and wander around in awe. Between May and August I take daily photographs just after sunrise to record flowering times and share the course of the summer with gardeners online, and this together with visiting horticultural groups and NGS open days sets the daily rhythm right through the summer. It is a delight to be able to share the beauty of the garden in full bloom with so many people, and to have a chance to step back and see it through their eyes. The days pass in a haze of sunrises and petals until suddenly it is late July and time to snap out of the dream and prune the fruit trees. Espaliered and fan-trained fruit trees grow all along the east face of the mirrored borders wall where they benefit from shelter and warmth, and the new growth needs to be shortened in high summer to create fruiting spurs. This is also the time to prune the long tendrils on the wisterias back to six buds, and these will be shortened again to two buds in December.

In August seed collecting begins in earnest. Every year I gather seeds from the self-sowing perennial species that grow around the garden and make them available for sale to visitors on open days and via my garden website. It is exciting to wander through the beds and see which plants are able to spare some seeds to start new lives in the world beyond the wall. By late August the mirrored borders are a picture of order and discipline, but in the rose garden the forest of new rose stems combined with a plethora of seedheads tips the balance more towards chaos. This is not helped by the distinctly shabby outlines of the box balls, so it is time for their annual haircut to restore order. There are 50 box balls around the garden of varying sizes, all grown from rooted cuttings planted between 2004 and 2009 and shaped by years of annual trimming with hand shears over a week in mid- to late August. They respond well to being trimmed at this time of year when the new season's growth has matured, and it is very rare that autumn is warm enough to trigger further growth, so they keep their pristine outlines right through the winter.

> The days pass in a haze of sunrises and petals until suddenly it is late July.

On the first day of September I put the camera away and get the ladders out, as it is time to start trimming the yew hedges – a slow and meticulous job that I really savour in the late summer sunshine. Together with the box balls, the precise lines of the yew hedges make an important contribution to the garden as a counterpoint to the billowing naturalistic style of the flowerbeds, and it is very rewarding to see them regain their disciplined outlines. Seed collecting continues right through September and into October, and along the kitchen garden wall the pear and apple harvest has begun.

This brings us at last to October, and as the apple and seed harvest continues, there are pumpkins and squash to cure in the sunshine before they come inside to be stored for the winter. With the trimmer mower back from its annual service and waiting at the stable door, it is time to lift all the delphinium supports out of the beds and return them to their winter quarters so that the cycle can begin again.

MY GARDEN TOOLS

I settled on the sequence of jobs through the year by a process of trial and error, but it is easy to overlook the vital contribution of the tools I use. The right tool for the job makes all the difference to the result, the time taken, and the impact on my joints, and in some cases I literally could not manage the garden on my own without them. My essential tools are as follows.

Joint supports: I use neoprene and velcro elbow, wrist, and back supports as a matter of course throughout the day, just as I wear shoes and a hat. They are an essential part of the job and I use them in different combinations to ensure I get everything done without compromising my fitness for the future. There was nothing wrong with my joints when I started this project, but looking ahead I could see that they would become my weakest link, and using joint supports to take the strain for all these years has protected them from damage.

Wheeled trimmer mower: this is the most important tool I have, and I could not maintain the garden in the time available without it. Using it is strenuous, noisy, and messy work, but it is so fast that I can fell the entire garden in just two weeks by using it for a couple of hours a day. Passing it over the fallen stems effectively gives me self-mulching flowerbeds, so when the job is done there is no raking up or carting away to do.

Soil rake: between January and March as the weather allows, I rake over the soil to loosen moss and check for perennial weeds. I use a regular soil rake, which is incredibly satisfying as it makes the job feel like grooming the garden with an enormous comb.

Rabbiting spade: this marvellous little spade has a much smaller, narrower head than a standard one, and the blade is rounded making it very easy to get into the soil. Despite its size I use it for all digging jobs, simply because it makes such light work of the task.

Mattock: this superb hand tool is two-sided with three prongs on one side and a flat bolster on the other, making it ideal for digging out deep-rooted weeds and preparing small planting holes. It is also handy for creating seed drills and then covering them over with soil in the vegetable garden.

Push-pull weeder: a long-handled weeder like a fixed stirrup hoe that works equally well on the out and back stroke, this indispensable tool has sharp wavy edges on the flat face and moulded corners ideal for nicking out weeds in tiny spaces. It is perfect for clearing large areas of weed seedlings and leaves the soil surface soft and crumbly.

Hori hori knife: this traditional Japanese tool looks like a cross between a dagger and a breadknife, and was originally used for winkling saplings out of crevices on rocky mountain slopes. The pointed end and serrated side make it useful for all sorts of gardening jobs, and it is perfect for teasing weeds out of perennial crowns.

Mulching lawnmower: my useful little walk-behind lawnmower is a quick and reliable tool for mowing edges and rough ground as it is designed to clear longer grass without leaving residue on the lawn. It is also very handy to have as back-up for the ride-on mower when it breaks down.

Ride-on lawnmower: I use a small ride-on mulching mower for the lawns and also for the area of grass outside the old stable block. After reliability problems with a larger ride-on mower, I replaced it with an entry-level model having realized I needed to be able to drag the machine off the lawn and out of the garden should it break down before visitors arrive. This entry-level mower works well and is light enough that I can move it on my own.

Edging shears and edging strip: the lawns here are all contained by a strong metal edging strip with teeth that has proved to be very durable, and it makes the edges very easy to trim by running edging shears along the metal as a guide.

String bundles: I use jute string around the garden but rather than carry the whole ball and scissors around with me, I tie pre-cut lengths into bundles and attach them to my belt. It is a great way to have an instant one-handed source of ties without fumbling around unwinding then trying to cut string while wrestling with plant stems.

Hand shears: old-fashioned hand shears are indispensable where precision matters, and I maintain them with frequent sharpening and lubricant. I use them to trim all the box balls in August and again to trim the yew hedges into shape in September, as well as on an ad hoc basis for other jobs throughout the year. They are very hard on the wrists and elbows, so I always ensure I use the appropriate joint supports.

Loppers and secateurs: I use ratchet loppers when pruning deciduous shrubs and thicker stems on the roses, and after many different brands of secateurs through the years, I settled on a Felco pair about 10 years ago. They are still as good as they day I bought them.

THE POWER OF CONSTRAINTS

One of the first decisions I made about the garden was what my constraints were going to be, because these had to be in place before I could make any meaningful decisions about anything else. Some were out of my hands, but others were deliberately self-imposed in order to harness their motivational and organizational power. The ancient Stoic phrase "memento mori" sums up the power of binding constraints: by remembering daily that I will die, I am motivated to treasure every day and make it really count. In the same way the constraints on a project throw focus onto the real value of the options that remain. Without them, opportunity is squandered, but with them, every opportunity becomes a challenge, a puzzle, and a game.

I am the biggest binding constraint on my garden because I have limited the scope of the project to what I can do alone: my motto is if I can't do it myself, then I can't do it at all. I made this decision because I view the garden as a source of activity rather than a possession, and I am naturally curious and driven to learn new things by trial and error. It made no sense at all to create a garden and hand the best part over to someone else, as that would be like buying a jigsaw puzzle and then hiring someone to do the puzzle for me. I limited the project to what I could achieve in five hours a day, year-round, because that was the amount of time spent watching television by the average person in the United Kingdom when I started out in 2003. I decided that if I was going to spend five hours a day escaping into a fantasy world, then it should at least be one of my own making, so I got rid of the television, moved my afternoon jobs to the evening, and allocated five hours in the afternoons to first designing, then creating, and finally maintaining the garden instead. At the time of writing, I have devoted 38,000 hours of my life to the garden, but the truly shocking thing is that I would have otherwise spent the same amount of time staring at the television. While I only have five hours a day for the garden, that constraint comes with the certainty of knowing that I do have those hours, so I can plan and allocate them most effectively when working out which jobs to do when throughout the year. As a lot of the work is strenuous, I find it extremely helpful to know that I only have to complete today's job today and that time has already been allocated for tomorrow's job tomorrow. This gives me the steadying hand needed to work on such a large project alone.

> My motto is if I can't do it myself, then I can't do it at all.

The garden is also bound by a long-term time constraint: I was 33 when I started this project and it was always my intention that the fate of the garden should mirror my own. At over 20 years old it is now fully mature, and while I haven't really noticed the effects of age, it is only natural that in the years ahead I will start to slow down, and one day it will be time for me to stop. I see the garden as rather like my snow angel – it is the imprint of my interactions with Mother Earth, and when I stop waving my arms around on the ground, I fully expect her to erase all trace of me.

I was keenly aware from the start that such a large and long-term project would need a very tight, strict budget if it was not going to turn into a financial nightmare, so I decided to stick to the cost of a Range Rover and a Freelander for the whole project. This seemed a good yardstick for a serious long-term commitment without being overly lavish or indulgent. I find a tight budget extremely motivating as it turns every decision into a challenge, and rather than throw money at a problem it stimulates me to innovate and come up with novel solutions. My decision to do all the gardening myself means that, excluding a payment to my neighbour's son who cuts the deciduous hedges, the garden's annual running costs are around £1,000, almost all of which goes on servicing and replacing garden machinery. During the setup phase of the garden, I did everything as cost effectively as possible by learning the skills and buying the raw materials wherever I reasonably could: my motto has always been do it yourself and you get a skill, hire someone else and you get a bill.

> The ultimate binding constraints on all gardeners are the climate and conditions of their plot.

The ultimate binding constraints on all gardeners are the climate and conditions of their plot, and I work within these gladly. One of the elements of my gardening system that generates a lot of interest among visitors is my strict no-watering policy. I grew up in West Sussex in the 1980s and witnessed the damage frequent hosepipe bans did, not just to people's gardens, tubs, and hanging baskets, but also to their morale and their relationship with their gardens. During hot weather their plants shrivelled but the surrounding countryside was still thriving, and I realized that the problem was water dependency, not water availability. As a result, with the exception of vegetable seedlings, I decided to implement a strict no-watering policy right from the start and create a place that was designed to survive unaided with only what the environment provided.

The decision not to water has far-reaching implications in the garden and leaves its mark on how and when I do certain jobs, what I can grow, and how to encourage plant health. Clearly drought tolerance becomes a key consideration in choosing what to grow, but that is just the start. There is no point in planting expensive pot-grown plants in late April and then just watching them die. Instead, growing plants from seed gave me an inexpensive way of sourcing large quantities and made me more sanguine about the inevitable losses. Not being able to water plants struggling to establish in hot weather rules out planting anything during the growing season. As a result, I limited myself to planting between 1st November and 1st March, and this means I can't grow tender perennials, half-hardy annuals, or bedding plants in the garden at all.

In the rose garden the decision not to water steered my choice of roses more towards the old varieties. My reasoning was that any rose widely grown long before the supply of mains water was more likely to have earned its spurs unaided. Tubs and baskets are incompatible with a no-watering regime, so they were never a feature here apart from a few small tubs of sempervivums, *Silene uniflora* that obligingly roots through the bottom of the pot, and an indestructible acer that has survived on rainwater for over 20 years. Something that I didn't consider was lawns. Once they turn brown the visual impact is immense, and the contrast between the overall look of the lawn-free rose garden and the mirrored borders after a heatwave is instructive. With hindsight I should have designed the garden with less lawn generally and certainly made it less prominent. With earlier and more intense heatwaves, this is sure to become a recurring issue in the future.

When heatwaves, drought, and a hosepipe ban coincided in 2022, it was fascinating to see how the self-sowing understorey in the rose garden held up. Having spent the previous 19 years being subjected to natural selection, the understorey had adapted incrementally over the years to increasingly harsh conditions. Anything that couldn't cope was already dead, so it sailed through completely unscathed. The following flowering plant species stood out as particularly heat- and drought-tolerant at the time:

Centrathus ruber	*Eryngium giganteum*	*Limonium platyphyllum*
Cephalaria gigantea	*Eryngium planum*	*Nepeta* x *faassenii*
Cichorium intybus	*Eupatorium cannabinum*	*Nepeta govaniana*
Cynara cardunculus	*Eupatorium purpureum*	*Perovskia atriplicifolia*
Echinops exaltatus	*Euphorbia characias*	*Romneya coulteri*
Echinops ritro	subsp. *wulfenii*	*Saponaria officinalis*
Echinops sphaerocephalus	*Foeniculum vulgare*	*Sedum spectabile*
Eryngium agavifolium	*Helleborus argutifolius*	*Sisyrinchium striatum*
Eryngium bourgatii	*Lavandula angustifolia*	
Eryngium eburneum	*Leucanthemum* x *superbum*	

Using binding constraints to come up with efficient ways to get the job done works in the same way as exposing the plants to the full force of nature to drive their adaptation: both myself and my plant populations use the discipline of constraints to improve how we achieve our goals. In order for this to work the constraints have to be sacrosanct, otherwise innovation is diverted into working out how to break through the constraints themselves rather than how to achieve goals within them. This is why I apply my rules across the board, without exception. No doubt there are many more, some so fundamental to my nature that I am completely unaware of how I build them into daily life, but I do know that for me binding constraints are an endless source of inspiration and motivation.

GOING SOLO

Garden visitors are often perplexed as to why I don't have any help in the garden. When I first started this project, all I knew about large gardens was that most of them founder due to labour costs, so initially I decided to restrict the project to what I could do on my own to make sure it didn't become a millstone with its fate always dependent on funds to pay gardeners. There was no garden here at all when I started and so no gardening work, and I also took the view that if I wasn't going to look after it, I had no business putting it on the ground in the first place. As it turned out there were so many benefits to going solo that it was not so much a constraint as a liberation.

An important part of the motivation for making and keeping the garden here is to create an opportunity for hands-on learning. I love learning by doing and the idea of a lifelong project with endless problems to solve is completely compelling. In our information and skills-dense world there are very few ways to encounter the limits of knowledge in daily life, so I engineer the spirit of discovery by reinventing the wheel. But keeping that spirit alive requires avoidance of anyone who might spoil the journey by telling me how it ends. Everyone has their own way of doing things, either gleaned from a preferred authority or from personal experience and I completely respect that, but my approach to the garden was to start from scratch. Everything had to be figured out methodically by trial and error, and in a system of this nature there is no room for dogmas and traditions, just lots of open-minded experimentation. In working things out for myself I deliberately wander off the beaten track to explore beyond the boundaries of my knowledge and challenge myself to come up with new solutions and ideas. The further I proceed the more individual and unique my journey becomes, and this is by necessity a solitary journey: anyone else would bring their own experience and expertise to bear and that influence would haul me back from my coalface.

We all form opinions about the competence of others and so naturally we take into consideration the impression we are making on those around us. This can be a good thing where it keeps us accountable and motivated, but it is a disaster when adopting trial and error and blue-sky thinking, as the last thing the process needs is premature judgements being made, be they real or imagined. Working alone insulates me from this pressure, leaving me free to make a real hash of something with the only consequence being a fit of giggles.

This garden stands and falls on my motivation as that is both the reason it exists in the first place and its Achilles heel. If I lose heart in the project and disengage it will quickly fall apart, so I am extremely aware and protective of what motivates me and why, and the drive to challenge myself and to seek my personal limits daily is a large part of this. The clarifying process of self-overcoming is the spark that gets me out of bed in the morning, so to pull me back from it would remove one of my main sources of motivation. There is nothing that gets me engaged as much as a challenge that is almost completely impossible – I am like a moth to a flame around them because success is so unlikely that I am totally robust to failure, but the benefits of success are worth any amount of struggle. Because of this anything I can do to add an extra element of challenge will always strengthen my motivation and commitment.

An important part of the appeal of gardening for me is the contemplative state of mind that comes with it, but to be so completely off guard and absorbed in the work really precludes being available to interact. When I am sure no-one will disturb me I hyperfocus, which involves transferring my awareness entirely into the project or problem I am working on. It feels like I step inside my own imagination and go to a distant shore, and this state is where I am most productive and peaceful but I can only get there if I am alone. As a result, I have always suspected that the best way to reach my goals is to limit them from the outset to what I can realistically achieve by myself. The peace, certainty, and reliability more than compensate for the burden of knowing there is no-one to help, and nobody can pull the rug out from under me if I'm not standing on one, so the risk of being let down is zero. Instead, I have the earth below, the sky above, nature all around, a song in my heart, and a list of interesting jobs in my back pocket. What more could I possibly ask for?

Countless tiny questions crop up in the garden every day and as I automatically consider, answer, and act on them while I work, they combine as brushstrokes on a canvas all made by the same hand. This very personal relationship with the garden would be completely shattered if the questions were answered by different people, or worse, not answered at all.

We are nearing the end of our journey together, but before we part I would like to share my approach to working with a blank canvas, and to being a blank canvas myself. For anyone new to gardening or considering creating a garden from scratch, I know first hand how daunting this can be and I hope that what follows will give you the confidence to make a start.

Chapter Eight

APPROACHING A BLANK CANVAS

Left: Turning abandoned ground into a thriving garden has been an intensely rewarding experience.

WHEN YOU ARE A BLANK CANVAS

Everyone has a preferred method for learning new things and I am happy to share here the approach that I used when making my garden, in the hope that it proves useful if you are just starting out on your own gardening adventures. There are of course numerous authoritative manuals and training courses that you can turn to, but one of the dangers when learning something new is that if you seek advice or follow an established authority, you will be drawn into existing schools of thought and lose sight of the full range of possibilities that are available to you. Even working out who to listen to is fraught with problems, as often there are as many different opinions as there are experts to hold them. Taking advice from someone can also leave you instructed but not enlightened, as without the thought process that brought them to their opinion you have no idea what to do if the instructions let you down except turn to a competing authority. For me, an approach that keeps possibilities alive and options open for longer is worth much more than one that follows an existing school of thought in search of confidence, so whenever I reasonably can, I figure things out by trial and error.

Designing and running experiments is independent, open-minded, relatively objective, and hugely engaging. As an approach, it offers all sorts of useable leads and lines of inquiry that have cropped up along the way, providing a wellspring of alternatives that do not drag you into extreme shifts in strategy. The ideal problem-solving approach is methodical and rigorous while remaining dispassionate about the outcome, and trial and error is just that. It takes a problem and runs it through a carding brush and with each stroke the nature of the eventual solution becomes clearer, and all the while emotion is channelled into the process rather than the outcome.

I usually start my experiments with three different methods to solve a problem, either randomly scavenged from the internet or whatever strikes me as sensible. First,

I try them simultaneously on a small scale to see which one shows the most promise, then I try three different versions of the best one, and so on in an iterative process that homes in on the eventual method of choice. Coming up with different ideas for methods and then inventing new versions of winning approaches is highly entertaining. It encourages innovative thinking in a way that learning from an outside source could never do, and it sets you on a path to developing deep practical understanding over the longer term.

Crucially, adopting trial and error gives you a way to make a meaningful start without requiring you to first learn a broad base of knowledge that is not directly relevant to the problems you are trying to solve. We are so used to associating knowledge with confidence that most people are very unsure of taking on a task without acquiring the know-how to do it first, but using a problem-solving strategy can be a far more objective, targeted, and practical way to find solutions in real time on the ground. Relying on an established authority also cuts you off from the coalface of new ideas, where only by finding and following your own leads can you hope to make progress. Trailblazers don't switch into that mode when they run out of well-worn paths to tread: they find their own path by choice even when established routes are freely available, and trial and error is a tool that works seamlessly both on and off the beaten track.

> It is only by putting things to the test that you can be sure you are starting from firm ground.

Tackling a project on your own with no training or experience will always be daunting and in the early stages you may be vulnerable to a loss of motivation. As disappointment is the result of frustrated expectations, anything that helps to define and manage those expectations is extremely valuable. I keep my expectations extremely low but plough on regardless, and because trial and error courts and requires failure in order to function, it is a fantastic mechanism for managing expectations when failure would otherwise be disheartening. Indeed, one of the reasons I try three different methods at once is so that my failures will always outweigh my successes. When the ideas that do not deliver are just as important to the process as the ones that do, the only way to truly fail would be to break the rules of the process rather than to come up with yet another idea that doesn't solve the problem.

It may seem inefficient or reckless to override conventional ways of doing things and pursue a problem-solving strategy that courts failure and reinvents the wheel, but traditions have a way of taking on a life of their own and it is only by putting things to the test that you can be sure you are starting from firm ground. A story about an old family recipe makes this point very well. The youngest in the family asked the recipe's originator why she cut the ends off a ham before cooking it. With each generation the presumed reason had become more elaborate and pivotal to success, but it turned out the real reason was because the great-grandmother's pot wasn't big enough! How often do we blindly follow methods that were originally chosen for reasons that are no longer relevant?

One of the appeals of gardening is the endless stream of interesting problems and challenges it generates, and by approaching it as an opportunity to experiment and be inventive, you can set off with a flexible, robust, and durable mindset that is ideally suited to the adventures ahead.

WHEN YOUR PLOT IS A BLANK CANVAS
Starting a new garden project from scratch is very exciting and its success depends on enthusiasm, but determination and patience are also key as a lot of messy and strenuous work lies ahead and it will take a few years for the vision to really take shape on the ground. When facing a blank canvas here, rather than charging headlong into the project, I found creating a scale layout and planting plan to be a very effective way to harness my enthusiasm and channel it into the long-term outcome. For each area of the garden I spent up to four months at the planning stage, and without the realistic grounding and steadying hand this gave me I would not have completed a single one. The planning process itself is also a useful test of commitment, as the time and effort involved will reveal whether the motivation is really there to create and look after the actual garden. During the growing season an incomplete project will be infested with weeds within weeks, so if the commitment to see it through is going to fade, it is better to find this out before starting any work on the ground.

To create my plans, I paced out the plot and drew it to scale on graph paper, and then I used separate tracing paper overlays for the layout and planting elements so that I could try a range of different options over the graph paper without marking it. Planning the layout on paper gave me a simple way to assess the impact of big-picture ideas on the lines of sight, routes, and distribution of structural elements around the garden, together with how they would look from different vantage points and relate to existing features. Once I was happy with the layout, I decided which flower categories to use, such as "white foam" or "blue spires", and assembled suitable candidates through internet searches, as described in Chapter Six. I compiled these into tables of plant options by flower colour, texture, height, growing conditions,

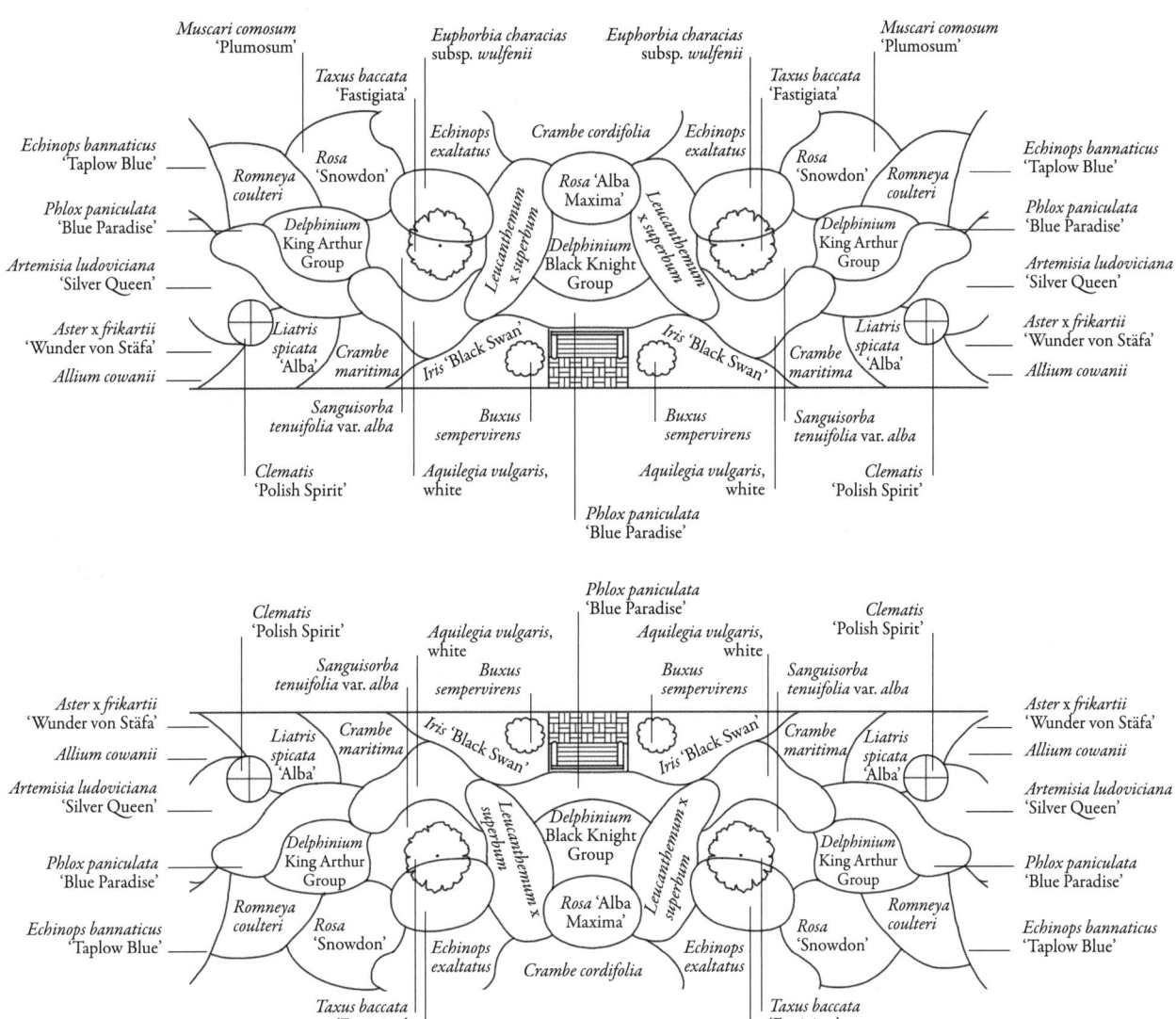

Above: A planting plan condenses months of research into a practical reference tool. This illustration shows the central section of my plan for the mirrored borders.

and flowering season. Then I selected plants from the tables as I filled in my planting overlay, referring to the graph paper beneath for a rough indication of scale.

Planting up flowerbeds is strenuous work so anything that increases the chances of getting it right first time is very worthwhile, and sitting in warmth and comfort surrounded by my plant tables meant that I could really give it my best shot. Working in this way kept a large number of options in mind for any particular spot, and taking the time to methodically decide what to plant where resulted in more thoughtful plant choices, which left a permanent trace on the ground. On a paper plan, assessing how flower colours would align across the bigger picture was very straightforward, as was checking how the garden would look at different times of year by highlighting plants that flower simultaneously. Figuring out how plants relate to each other and considering different options was a very enjoyable and creative process for its own

APPROACHING A BLANK CANVAS

sake, so once the planting plan was complete, I laminated it – as much to draw the decision-making process to a definitive close as to protect it from mud and rain.

Garden visitors often ask how many individual plants I used per patch when laying out a new flowerbed, and this was determined entirely by the area it covered on my planting plan. Because I think of the garden as a collage made with living components, the number of plants only became relevant when it was time to grow or source them. At that point I laid my tracing paper plan back over the graph paper and read off the exact area to work out how many I needed for each patch, which was anything from three to 20 individual plants.

> It takes enthusiasm to start a garden project from scratch but endurance to finish one.

Having a scale layout plan really gives you the confidence to start work on the ground, otherwise it is very difficult to make the leap from ideas and sketches to knowing precisely what to do where. It can be hard to stay motivated during projects with a lot of up-front effort and delayed rewards, and the plan acts as a valuable route map where otherwise it could be easy to lose sight of the reason for all the mud and struggle. It is also a very useful communication tool, as creating a garden is bound to invite comment from neighbours, family, and friends and it is fortifying to be able to show them that despite the apparent chaos, the project really is on firm ground.

As work progresses to the planting stage, the plan is vital for keeping things on track, particularly when plant availability is staggered as may be the case when you are propagating them yourself. While I was planting up the mirrored borders, it took me three years to propagate all the home-grown plants, and over that time the planting plan worked just like the picture on a jigsaw-puzzle box. During the long process of filling in the empty spaces, it was very reassuring to know that the vision was already fixed and permanent, rather than to feel, as the months passed by, that it was gradually slipping away.

It may sound dull to start a new garden project by spending weeks at the kitchen table, but the planning process gave me a realistic sense of the job I was taking on and an opportunity to make endless mistakes on paper. The plans themselves were invaluable for keeping the project on course – so much so that I would never start work on the ground without them. It takes enthusiasm to start a garden project from scratch but endurance to finish one, and having a fully formed blueprint of the end goal will give you the guidance and motivation necessary to reach it.

Left: The planting plan will keep your vision alive while you turn it into a reality.

CONCLUSION

Right: Self-sown wildflowers add diversity and elegance to the pastels garden beds.

The ability to modify our environment is a striking feature of our species, but while it is responsible for some of our greatest achievements, it also has the power to alienate us from the natural world. Water comes from a tap, light from a switch, food from a shop, and we are so used to technology being the solution to every problem that it is easy to presume it has removed our dependency on the planet's natural systems. Somewhere between the layers of production, commerce, marketing, and logistics that separate consumers from the source of raw materials, the link between the two has been lost – even to the point where we hear of people who genuinely believe that what happens in the countryside doesn't matter because their food is made in a factory. I am convinced this alienation is at the root of our antagonistic relationship with the environment. We approach it as an afterthought and a source of frustration, rather than recognising that how we relate to it may be wrong-headed in the first place.

We only have to look at the consequences for the climate to see that this drive to differentiate ourselves from nature and then to dominate it is running out of road. For one species to believe itself to be outside of the web of life on its own planet is foolish beyond belief, and this drive has taken us so far that alienation from the natural world is now a greater source of danger than the wilderness we set out to tame. In gardening we have elevated our environment-modifying behaviour to an art form. If our gardens can show that being embedded in nature is a positive thing, if they can demonstrate that operating within the boundaries of natural systems does not mean giving up what we hold dear, then they can lead the way in forging a more respectful and co-operative relationship with the natural world.

There is no inherent conflict of interests between the garden and the environment any more than there is between your nose and your face: one is just a small part of the

> For one species to believe itself to be outside of the web of life on its own planet is foolish.

CONCLUSION

other. The conflict only comes about when another agenda steps between the two, such as the goal of growing three perfect matching blooms, or the desire to protect new additions to a flowerbed planted during the heat of summer. It is unrealistic expectations that introduce the conflict, and my experience here has shown that by tweaking gardening practices and priorities so that they operate within the constraints of natural systems, the conflict melts away. Gardening continually prompts us to reconsider our relationship with nature, and by accepting and investing in our role as custodians of the environment and acting in the interests of the system rather than protecting a few chosen individuals, we can avoid our decisions being skewed by conflicts fabricated entirely by ourselves. We need to take a step back, to garden in a way that lets nature make more of the decisions, and not pride ourselves according to the yardsticks of a bygone age but instead focus on how well we treat the natural world, and on how much we can achieve by harnessing natural systems instead of opposing them.

> We need to take a step back, to garden in a way that lets nature make more of the decisions.

Welcoming the ecosystem into the garden means being in the presence of the raw power of nature and this is a very humbling experience. Being surrounded by the energy and vitality of my garden is intensely elevating, but it leaves no room for ego or self-importance. It is all I dare hope for that Mother Nature doesn't wipe me out with a single swipe of her paw, and with that humility comes gratitude for the blessing of living on this enchanting planet – something that is so often taken for granted. In our relationship with our little plot each of us has a chance to coexist with a power far greater than ourselves, and to engage respectfully with something beyond our control.

> In our relationship with our little plot each of us has a chance to coexist with a power far greater than ourselves, and to engage respectfully with something beyond our control.

We have used our inventiveness to tame the wilds, and now it is time to put that inventiveness to a new purpose and figure out how to achieve our goals by harnessing natural processes rather than defying them. When we lose our way, we need to retrace our steps to a place from where we can move forward again with confidence, and in my experiments here I have been trying to do just that.

By starting with observations in the countryside to bring the full range of possibilities back into consideration, I have been constructing new ways of thinking about relating to nature and gardening, and deciding what goals are achievable in the garden. In particular I have been trying to understand the nature of the balance between

CONCLUSION

wilderness and a cultivated environment, and then to bring elements of both together in different combinations to see what happens. By figuring out which elements trigger the feeling of gardenhood, I aimed to apply only those that are essential to produce a garden that looks and feels like a very human environment but functions as much like a wilderness as possible. By growing hardy perennial species as self-sowing populations with no interference, I managed to harness natural selection so that my garden can adapt to changing conditions while at the same time providing the habitat necessary for a healthy food chain.

> I managed to harness natural selection so that my garden can adapt to changing conditions while at the same time providing the habitat necessary for a healthy food chain.

Starting with a blank canvas gave me an opportunity to work at the systems level rather than having to steer an existing garden into a new regime piecemeal. Because of my love for the woodlands and my way of life here, I understood that the best way to access natural systems was to go back to their source instead of tinkering at the edges of established gardening practices. Learning how to garden in nature's slipstream has been analogous to befriending a wolf rather than teaching new tricks to a spaniel. To succeed, this required an approach based on observation, acceptance, humility, and respect rather than one based on ownership, dominance, and control. By sharing some of the observations, methods, and techniques I developed on my journey in from the wild side, I hope that together we can strike a new balance between the gardener and the environment that accommodates the needs of both.

Every garden faces different challenges and no-one has a crystal ball regarding what will come our way in the years ahead, but I hope you will be persuaded by my experiments to believe that it is possible to produce a healthy, dynamic, and beautiful garden that thrives under the iron rule of natural systems. More than anything I hope you will be inspired to begin experiments of your own. I started with a scruffy field in the middle of nowhere and harnessed the power of nature to bring my garden into existence, and I am sure that you can do the same. Even if you commit just a small area of your garden to self-sowing perennial species, you will be amazed by the difference in plant health, adaptability, diversity, and wildlife compared to a traditional flowerbed, and who knows where it might lead?

> More than anything I hope you will be inspired to begin experiments of your own.

My binding constraints limit my project to only what I can maintain myself, so I had to stop creating new garden areas to care for those I had already made, but there are so many more experiments that I could have done and would love to see happen. An ornamental ecosystem of self-sowing perennial species that combines a restricted colour scheme with successional planting would be a superb project, resulting in an evolving climate-friendly and climate-change-ready garden full of wildlife with a stable and enduring character and a very long flowering season.

Another experiment that suggests itself is to start out with a combination of species and their named varieties with a very wide range of characteristics, in an attempt to increase the diversity among their seedlings. This would be particularly valuable to both pollinators and the gardener if it generated a wider spread of flowering times. From a more aesthetic perspective, another project would be the genetic equivalent of slow-motion watercolour painting: named varieties within each species could be planted in such a way that over time their seedlings merge the colours of the initial plants in swathes across the flowerbeds as a living testament to the movements of the foraging insects that pollinated them.

> We are wired to seek out Eden, to long for idealized places, things, and people, yet in the wild places on our planet and in our gardens, we are already there.

It would also be a fascinating experiment to combine a garden's livery and layout so that they create strong visual containment for a community of perennial species selected entirely from native wildflowers, with meticulously trained wild roses and obelisks of wild honeysuckle. The combination of the two extremes could be electrifying, and presenting wild plants in a manner traditionally associated with horticultural excellence would reframe them as the treasures they already are. The possibilities are almost endless, but I can't do this by myself. I need you to take it from here and set up an ornamental ecosystem of your own so that your garden too can become part of this wonderful experiment.

There is nothing more profoundly moving, more nourishing on an emotional, spiritual, and intellectual level, than standing in my rose garden surrounded by the diversity and energy of life and knowing that I am in the midst of evolution in action. I am actually witnessing it in real time, and the intensity and sense of connection are unparalleled. We are wired to seek out Eden, to long for idealized places, things, and people, yet in the wild places on our planet and in our gardens, we are already there. The way we see the world is veiled by our projections, and if we trample our true Eden in pursuit of our illusions of it, then we are doomed to eternally seeking but never reaching a sustainable relationship with our only home.

In our relationship with the planet each of us assumed we were just a drop in the ocean, but it turned out instead that we are the ocean in a single drop. We are members of a social species but each of us is something so much more than this: we are a small part of the biosphere connecting the earth to the sky, and focusing on each other to the exclusion of that will be our undoing. We all have to make our own peace with the planet, and how we relate to it has nothing to do with how other people, nations, or continents behave and everything to do with the respect and gratitude that we hold in our own hearts. What you do matters. You matter. Through the thousands of individual choices we made in the past, we have already proved that we have the power to bring about planet-scale change, and our gardens are the perfect place to own that power and use it for good.

MAP OF THE GARDEN

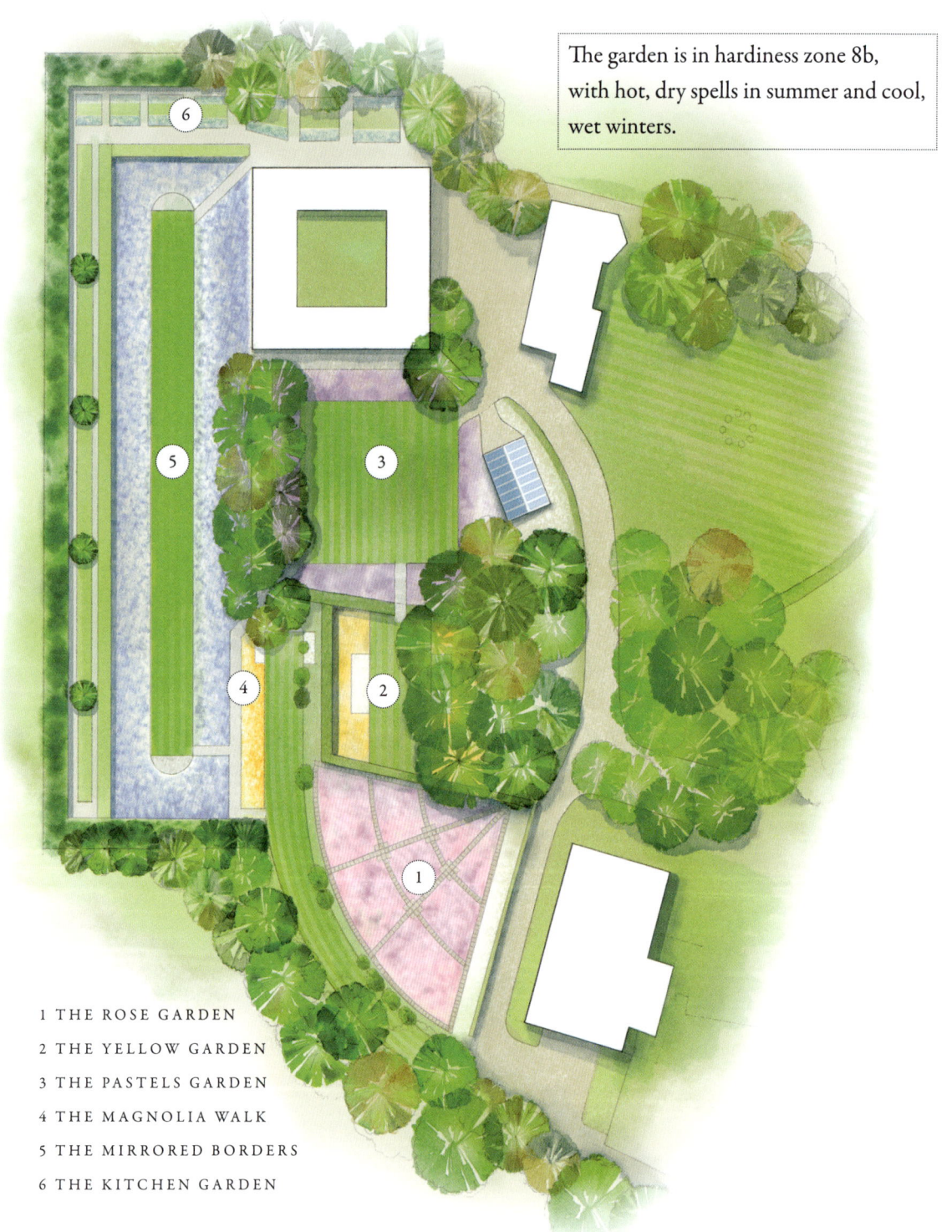

The garden is in hardiness zone 8b, with hot, dry spells in summer and cool, wet winters.

1 THE ROSE GARDEN
2 THE YELLOW GARDEN
3 THE PASTELS GARDEN
4 THE MAGNOLIA WALK
5 THE MIRRORED BORDERS
6 THE KITCHEN GARDEN

INDEX

Page numbers in *italics* refer to illustrations

A
acer 199
Achillea 'Appleblossom' 178, *179*
   A. 'Inca Gold' 180, *181*
Aconitum carmichaelii 'Arendsii' 160, *161*, 186
   A. napellus 160, *161*
   A. n. subsp. *vulgare* 'Albidum' 156, *157*
Agapanthus 'Headbourne White' 186
ailing plants 83
Alchemilla 144, 169
   A. mollis 61, 85, 99, *99*, 172, *173*
Allium 26, 64
   A. cowanii 67, 164, *165*
   A. cristophii 85, 100, *100*, 162, *163*
   A. giganteum 172, *173*
   A. hollandicum 17
   A. neapolitanum Cowanii Group 164, *165*
   A. nigrum 67, 164, *165*
Althaea officinalis 178, *179*
Amelanchier lamarckii 30
Amsonia tabernaemontana var. *salicifolia* 166, *167*
Anaphalis triplinervis 178, *179*
Andersen, Hans Christian, *The Little Mermaid* 71
Anemone × *hybrida* 'Honorine Jobert' 174, *175*
   A. nemorosa 176, *177*
animals 92–93
Anthriscus sylvestris 101, *101*, 176, *177*
apples 74, 194
apricots 74, 93
April jobs 193
Aquilegia vulgaris var. *stellata* 'Ruby Port' 180, *181*
Artemisia 70, 145
   A. ludoviciana 'Silver Queen' 174, *175*, 178, *179*

artichokes 93
Asplenium scolopendrium 176, *177*
Aster 70, 155
   A. × *frikartii* 'Wunder von Stäfa' 166, *167*, 174, *175*, 183
Astilbe 158, *159*
Astrantia 64
   A. 'Hadspen Blood' 180, *181*
   A. major 85, *94*, 102, *102*
August jobs 193, 194

B
badgers 93
bearded irises 68
beech hedges 61, 62, 186
bees 93
birds 92–93
blackbirds 92
blackcurrants 74
blackthorn 140
Bladbean 7, 138
blank canvases 202–09, 213
   plots as a blank canvas 206–09
   you as a blank canvas 204–06
boldness 149
box
   box balls 68, *69*, 70, 81, 143, 190, *191*, 194
   maintaining 194, 196
   repeating motifs 143
   trimming, 194
brambles 192
Buddleja alternifolia 30
budgets 198
bulbs
   in bountiful colour scheme 180, *181*
   in mellow colour scheme 172, *173*
   in nostalgic colour scheme 178, *179*
   in refreshing colour scheme 176, *177*
   in tranquil colour scheme 174, *175*

bumblebees 93
Buxus sempervirens 68

C
Camassia 64
   C. leichtlinii 'Alba' 103, *103*, 156, *157*
   C. l. subsp. *suksdorfii* Caerulea Group 160, *161*
Campanula 64
   C. alliariifolia 176, *177*
   C. lactiflora 63, 85, 104, *104*, 166, *167*, 174, *175*
   C. persicifolia 105, *105*
Catananche caerulea 166, *167*, 178, *179*, 184
Centaurea macrocephala 61, 105, *105*
   C. montana 85, 106, *106*
Centranthus ruber 199
   C. r. 'Albus' 67, 85, 107, *107*, 164, *165*
Cephalaria gigantea 67, 108, *108*, 172, *173*, 199
chaffinches 93
Chamaenerion angustifolium 'Album' 114, *114*, 156, *157*
cherries 74
Cichorium intybus 108, *108*, 199
Clematis 68
   C. 'Blue Angel' 174, *175*
climate 198
   climate change 8, 78, 210
climbers
   in bountiful colour scheme 180, *181*
   in mellow colour scheme 172, *173*
   in nostalgic colour scheme 178, *179*
   in refreshing colour scheme 176, *177*
   in tranquil colour scheme 174, *175*
colour
   avoiding unintended colour clashes 170
   leaf colour 144

colour schemes
    blue billows 166, *167*
    blue, silver, and white 147
    blue spires 160, *161*
    bountiful colour scheme 180, *181*
    mellow colour scheme 172, *173*
    nostalgic colour scheme 178, *179*
    pink clouds 158, *159*
    refreshing colour scheme 176, *177*
    restricted colour schemes 79
    sample restricted colour schemes 171–81
    tranquil colour scheme 174, *175*
    violet haze 162, *163*
    white foam 164, *165*
    white spires 156, *157*
compromise 149
constraints
    power of constraints 196–99
    working within binding constraints 16, 18, 213
cornflowers 106, *106*
Corylus avellana 176, *177*
countryside, as a source of design ideas 138–49, 212
cow parsley 140
creative palettes 148
Crocosmia × *crocosmiiflora* 'Honey Angels' 180, *181*
Cynara cardunculus 70, 109, *109*, 172, *173*, 199

D
Daedalus (Greek mythology) 71
David Austin Roses 32, 54–59, 61
    Rosa 'The Alnwick Rose' 57, *57*
    R. 'Barbara Austin' 58, *58*
    R. 'Constance Spry' 56, *56*
    R. 'John Clare' 54, *54*
    R. 'Mary Rose' 56, *56*
    R. 'The Mayflower' 59, *59*
    R. 'A Shropshire Lad' 55, *55*
    R. 'Winchester Cathedral' 59, *59*
deadheading, gardening without 64, 81, 87, 89, 90, 190
    benefits of 82
December jobs 192
Delphinium 26, 68, 88
    D. elatum 156, *157*, 160, *161*
    supports 193, 194

design observations 136–51
    finding your own style 148–51
    scale, journey, and destination 141–43
    through the lens 143–48
design process 19–23
design techniques 152–87
    restricted colour schemes 168–87
    scale layouts and planting plans 206–209, *207*
    successional blooming in fixed roles 154–67
destination 141–43
Digitalis ferruginea 180, *181*
    D. grandiflora 176, *177*
    D. lutea 61, 110, *110*
    D. purpurea 64, *64*
    D. p. f. *albiflora* 61, 86, 111, *111*, 156, *157*, 176, *177*
Dipsacus fullonum 178, *179*
diseases 18, 31, 81, 91, 190
drought 199

E
Echinacea 'Harvest Moon' 180, *181*
    E. purpurea 112, *112*
Echinops 64, 70
    E. exaltatus 85, 174, *175*, 199
    E. ritro 85, 112, *112*, 178, *179*, 199
    E. sphaerocephalus 113, *113*, 199
Echo (Greek mythology) 71
Eden 8, 214
edging shears 196
edging strip 196
elements, visible and highly manicured 79–81
emotions 19
enchanted glades 140–41
The English Garden 11
Epilobium 64
    E. angustifolium 'Album' 85, 114, *114*, 156, *157*, 176, *177*
Eryngium 64, 70
    E. agavifolium 115, *115*, 199
    E. bourgatii 116, *116*, 166, *167*, 174, *175*, 199
    E. eburneum 116, *116*, 199
    E. giganteum 86, 117, *117*, 178, *179*, 199
    E. planum 118, 199
    E. variifolium 178, *179*

Eupatorium cannabinum 158, *159*, 199
    E. purpureum 199
Euphorbia 64, 144, 169
    E. amygdaloides var. *robbiae* 176, *177*
    E. characias subsp. *wulfenii* 199
experiments, designing and running 204–06

F
February jobs 192–93
Filipendula rubra 158, *159*
    F. ulmaria 164, *165*
financial constraints 198
flowerbeds, adapting existing 87–90
flowering season, extending 182–87
focal points 79, *80*, 143
Foeniculum vulgare 172, *173*, 180, *181*, 199
forest trails 29
foxgloves 140, *152*
    Digitalis lutea 61, 110, *110*
    D. purpurea 64, *64*
    D. p. f. *albiflora* 61, 86, 111, *111*, 156, *157*
framing 147
fruit trees 194

G
garden rooms 170
Gardeners' World, BBC 11
gardening year 190–201
geometry 79
Geranium 26, 64
    G. pratense 67, *187*
    G. p. var. *pratense* f. *albiflorum* 61, 85, 119, *119*
    G. sylvaticum 119, *119*
glades, enchanted 140–41
globe thistles 112–13, *112*, *113*
grape vines 75
Greek myths 71
growing conditions, no interference in 81

H
hand shears 196
hard landscaping 79
harebells 105, *105*
hawkbit 140
hawthorn 140

INDEX

heatwaves 199
hedges 81, 138, 198
   beech hedges 61, 62, 186
   privet hedges 186
   yew hedges 190, 194, 196
height 147
Helleborus argutifolius 199
Hemerocallis 'Corky' 180, *181*
   H. 'Stafford' 180, *181*
herbaceous plants
   in bountiful colour scheme 180, 181
   in mellow colour scheme 172, 173
   in nostalgic colour scheme 178, 179
   in refreshing colour scheme 176, 177
   in tranquil colour schemes 174, 175
   strimming 192
Hibiscus 30
hoeing 190
hogweed 140
holistic system 16–25
hori hori knife 196
horizontal lines 147
hosepipe bans 198, 199
Humulus lupulus 176, *177*
Hyacinthoides non-scripta 'Alba' 176, *177*
Hydrangea 'Annabelle' 70
   H. petiolaris 186
Hylotelephium cauticola 186
   H. spectabile 129, *129*, 164, *165*

I

Icarus (Greek mythology) 71
immersion 141
innovation 16–18, 19
Inula magnifica 180, *181*
Iris
   bearded iris 68
   Iris 'Kent Pride' 180, *181*
   I. 'Lemon Ice' 172, *173*
   I. 'Sable' 172, *173*
   I. 'White City' 174, *175*
   I. 'Winter Olympics' *152*
Irish yew *69*, *146*, *191*

J

January jobs 192
joint supports 195
journey 141–43
July jobs 193–94
June jobs 193–94
jute string 196

K

kitchen garden 74–75, *216*
Knautia arvensis 64, 85, 121, *121*
knowledge, gaining 204–06
Kolkwitzia amabilis 30

L

Lamprocapnos spectabilis 'Alba' 176, *177*
Lavandula angustifolia 199
lawnmowers 196
lawns 79, 81
   mowing 190, 196
   no-watering scheme 199
layers, repeating 140
layout 79
   scale layouts 206–09, *207*
   in winter 148
leaf colour 144
Leucanthemum × *superbum* 61, 67, 120, *120*, 199
   L. vulgare 64, 85
light and shade 144
Limonium platyphyllum 67, 121, *121*, 162, *163*, 199
lines of sight 79, *80*
loppers 196
lupins 156, *157*, 160, *161*

M

Magnolia × *loebneri* 'Leonard Messel' 67
magnolia walk 66–67, *216*
maintenance 190–95
   annual cycle of jobs 192–94
   tools 195–96
Malva moschata 85, 122, *122*
March jobs 190, 192, 193, 198
mass planting 141
Matteuccia struthiopteris 176, *177*
mattock 195
May jobs 193–94
meadow cranesbill 119, *119*
mirrored borders 68–73, 140, 142–43, 147, 148, *150–51*, 154, 169, 174, 190, *191*, 193, 194, 209, *216*
   colour schemes 169, 174
   design and layout 68, 70–71, 142–43, 147, 148, *150–51*
   maintenance 190, 193, 194
   planting 68–70, 209
   successional blooming 154
mood 169
Moorhouse, Pete, *Angel* sculpture 30
moss 192, 195
motifs, repeating 143–44
mulch 192
mulching lawnmower 196

N

Narcissus (Greek mythology) 71
National Garden Scheme (NGS) 10, 11, 61, 193
nature, respecting 16
Nemesis (Greek mythology) 71
Nepeta × *faassenii* 166, *167*, 187, 199
   N. govaniana 199
nettles 192
November jobs 190, 192, 198

O

observation 182
October jobs 194
Old Bladbean Stud Gardens
   design process 19–23
   ethos behind 16–19
   garden tour 26–75
   history and future of the garden 23–25
   map of the garden *216*
   origins of 7–11
olive trees 74–75
orchids 140
organic matter 18, 190, 192
Origanum vulgare 64
ornamental ecosystems 83–85, 170, 214
ox-eye daisies *63*

P

Passiflora caerulea 178, *179*
pastels garden 62–65, 67, *211*, *216*
   design and layout 62, 148
   maintenance 64

INDEX

paths 141
  curved paths *139*, 140, 143
  pressure-washing 193
  straight paths 143
peaches 74
pears 74, 194
perennials 81, 213
  adapting existing flowerbeds 87–90
  growing from seed 94–98
  self-sowing understorey *80*, 85–87, 90, 171, 194, 199
  species that self-sow 97–135
Perovskia atriplicifolia 199
  P. a. 'Blue Spire' 166, *167*
Persicaria campanulata 158, *159*
pests 18, 31, 81, 190
Phlomis italica 178, *179*
  P. russeliana 61, 123, *123*, 172, *173*
Phlox paniculata 164, *165*
  P. paniculata 'Mount Fuji' 174, *175*
Phuopsis stylosa 85, 124, *124*, 158, *159*
pigeons 92
planting
  mass planting and restricted range of plants 141
  planting plans 206–09, *207*
  successional blooming in fixed roles 154–67
  successional planting 140
  three storeys of planting 138
plants
  adventurous plant choices 170
  ailing plants 83
  choosing 22, 170, 185–86
  mingling plant populations 82
  undisturbed plant communities 82–83
plots
  blank canvases 206–209
  plot conditions 198
plums 74
pollinators 92, *97*, 214
poppies *75*
Primula vulgaris 176, *177*
priorities, changing 90–91
privet hedges 186
problem solving 204–06
pruning 194, 196
pumpkins 75, 194
push-pull weeder 195

R
rabbiting spade 195
rakes 195
raking 190, 192
reactions, studying your 148
red valerian 107, *107*
redcurrants 74
refreshing colour schemes 176, *177*
rewilding 78
Rheum palmatum 180, *181*
ride-on lawnmowers 196
Romneya coulteri 199
roses 26
  alba roses 46–48, 61
  Bourbon roses 38–41
  damask roses 52–53
  David Austin varieties 54–59, 61
  gallica roses 49–51
  hybrid musks 42–43, 61
  moss roses 44–5
  old rose varieties 31, 32, *33*, 34
  pruning 31, 32, 192, 196
  rugosa hybrids 34–37
  supports for 193
  training 190, 192
Rosa 'Adam Messerich' 41, *41*
  R. × 'Alba Maxima' 47, *47*
  R. 'Alba Semiplena' 48, *48*
  R. 'Albertine' 57
  R. 'The Alnwick Rose' 57, *57*
  R. 'Barbara Austin' 58, *58*
  R. 'Belle Poitevine' 37, *37*
  R. 'Blarii Number Two' 39, *39*
  R. 'Buff Beauty' 42, *42*
  R. 'Celestial' 46, *46*
  R. 'Chapeau de Napoléon' 44, *44*
  R. 'Charles de Mills' 51, *51*
  R. 'Climbing Souvenir de la Malmaison' 38, *38*
  R. 'Constance Spry' 56, *56*
  R. 'Coupe d'Hébé' 39, *39*
  R. 'Duchesse de Montebello' 51, *51*
  R. gallica var. *officinalis* 49, *49*
  R. 'Gypsy Boy' *33*, 40, *40*
  R. 'Hansa' 37, *37*
  R. 'Henri Martin' *33*, 45, *45*
  R. 'Honorine de Brabant' 41, *41*
  R. 'Hunter' 36, *36*
  R. 'Ispahan' 52, *52*
  R. 'John Clare' 54, *54*
  R. 'Königin von Dänemark' 47, *47*
  R. 'La Ville de Bruxelles' 53, *53*
  R. 'Louise Odier' 38, *38*
  R. 'Madame Hardy' 53, *53*
  R. 'Madame Lauriol de Barny' 39, *39*
  R. 'Maiden's Blush' 48, *48*
  R. 'Martin Frobisher' 35, *35*
  R. 'Mary Rose' 56, *56*, 59
  R. 'The Mayflower' 59, *59*
  R. 'Pax' 43, *43*
  R. 'Président de Sèze' 50, *50*
  R. 'Prosperity' 43, *43*
  R. 'Roseraie de l'Haÿ' 35, *35*
  R. 'A Shropshire Lad' 55, *55*
  R. 'Snowdon' 36, *36*
  R. 'Thérèse Bugnet' 34, *34*
  R. 'Tuscany Superb' 50, *50*
  R. 'William Lobb' 45, *45*
  R. 'Winchester Cathedral' 59, *59*
rose garden 23, 29–59, 70, 71, 85–87, 142, 143, *168*, 169, *188*, 193, 194, 199, *216*
  colour schemes 169
  design and layout 142, 143
  growing conditions 30
  history and future of 23
  layout 29–30
  maintenance *188*, 193, 194
  no-watering policy 199
  planting, pruning, and training roses 30–33
  rose varieties 30, 32, 34–59
rosebay willowherb 114, *114*, 140, 156, *157*
Ruta graveolens 172, *173*

S
Salvia 70
  S. 'Blue Spire' 166, *167*
  S. nemorosa 125, *125*
  S. sclarea var. turkestanica 178, *179*
  S. verticillata 67, 85, 126, *126*, 162, *163*
Sanguisorba 70
  S. obtusa 158, *159*
  S. officinalis 180, *181*
  S. tenuifolia var. *alba* 127, *127*, 155, 164, *165*, 174, *175*

Saponaria officinalis 85, 128, *128*, 158, *159*, 199
scabious 108, *108*
scale, in and of gardens 141–43, 147
   scale layouts 206–9, *207*
sea holly 115–18, *115–18*
seasons, extending the flowering season in an existing garden 182–87
secateurs 196
Sedum 64, 70
   S. cauticola 186
   S. spectabile 129, *129*, 164, *165*, 199
   S. s. 'Iceberg' 174, *175*
seeds
   collecting seeds 194
   growing perennials from 94–135, 198
   welcoming wildlife with 92
self-sowing perennials 82, 83, 97–135
   seed collection 194
   self-sowing understorey *80*, 85–87, 90, 171, 194, 199
sempervivums 199
September jobs 194
shade and light 144
shears
   edging shears 196
   hand shears 196
shrubs 192
   in bountiful colour scheme 180, *181*
   in mellow colour scheme 172, *173*
   in nostalgic colour scheme 178, *179*
   in refreshing colour scheme 176, *177*
   in tranquil colour scheme 174, *175*
   pruning 196
sight, lines of 79, *80*
Silene uniflora 130, *130*, 199
Sisyrinchium 64
   S. striatum 61, 130, *130*, 199
sky 138
soil, bare 82, 144
sowing seeds *see* self-sowing perennials
spade, rabbiting 195
spring-cleaning jobs 193
squash 75, 194
squirrels 93
Stachys byzantina 178, *179*
stems, dead 90, 190, 192
Stipa gigantea 180, *181*

Stokesia laevis 'Träumeri' 178, *179*
storeys 138
   self-sowing understorey *80*, 85–87, 90, 171, 194, 199
string bundles 196
structure, in winter 148
style, finding your own 148–51
successional planting 140
   successional blooming in fixed roles 154–67
Succisa pratensis 64, 85, 131, *131*, 162, *163*
sunflowers 75, *75*, 93
sweetcorn 75, *75*, 93
Symphyotrichum ericoides 'Pink Cloud' 158, *159*
   S. 'Little Carlow' 166, *167*, 174, *175*, 186
Syringa 30

T
Taxus baccata 'Fastigiata' 61, 68
Teucrium scorodonia 85, 132, *132*, 176, *177*
Thalictrum 64
   T. aquilegiifolium 158, *159*, 162, *163*
   T. delavayi 162, *163*, 172, *173*
   T. rochebruneanum 133, *133*, 162, *163*
tiers, repeating 140
time constraints 197–98
tools 195–96
topiary 190, 194
transitions, narrow 138, 142
transplanting 96
trees
   fruit trees 194
   in bountiful colour scheme 180, *181*
   in mellow colour scheme 172, *173*
   in nostalgic colour scheme 178, *179*
   in refreshing colour scheme 176, *177*
   in tranquil colour scheme 174, *175*
   olive trees 74–75
   yew trees 61, 68, *69*, *146*, *191*
trial and error 205–06
Trillium grandiflorum 176, *177*
trimmer mowers 192, 195
tubs 199
twilight zone 147

U
understorey, self-sowing perennial *80*, 85–87, 90, 171, 194, 199

V
Valeriana officinalis 85, 134, *134*, 164, *165*
vegetables 193
Verbascum chaixii 'Album' 67, 85, 135, *135*, 156, *157*
   V. thapsus (biennial) 172, *173*
Verbena bonariensis 162, *163*
Veronica gentianoides 160, *161*
   V. longifolia 160, *161*
Veronicastrum 70
   V. virginicum 160, *161*, 174, *175*
   V. v. 'Album' 156, *157*, 178, *179*
   V. v. 'Fascination' 172, *173*
Viburnum 30
views
   focal points 79, *80*, 143
   signature views 143

W
watering, no-watering policy 18, 81, 87, 89, 96, 198–99
weeder, push-pull 195
weeding 89–90, 190, 192, 193, 195, 196
Weigela 30
white, effects in the garden 144
whitecurrants 74
wild angelica 140
wildflowers 85, 92, 140, *211*, 214
wildlife 83, 154
   welcoming 92–93
winter, structure and layout in 148
wisteria 67, 194
woodlands 176, 213
working alone 200–01

Y
yellow garden 60–61, *216*
   rose varieties in 61
yew 144, *146*
   Irish yew *69*, *146*, *191*
   yew hedges 190, 194, 196
   yew trees 61, 68, *69*, *146*, *191*

AUTHOR'S ACKNOWLEDGMENTS

To my mum, your open-minded tolerance and loyalty have been the bedrock of my life, and I would be a very different person without them. Thank you for raising me to think for myself and to follow my own star.

To Maitland, thank you for all your support and encouragement in the garden's early years and for being such an important part of my life's journey, and to Jonathan, thank you for breaking me out of the woods and shepherding me back into the modern world. No-one else could have done it, and without your friendship I simply would not have written this book.

Thank you to my wonderful Facebook followers for your tireless encouragement and companionship, and to everyone who has visited the garden over the years – it has been a joy to meet you all. Every one of you has contributed something to this book by allowing me to see the garden through your eyes.

Thanks also to Richard Stileman for detailed advice and enthusiastic feedback on the manuscript, to Helen Griffin at RHS Books for running an expert eye over the manuscript, and to Clive Nichols for reading and commenting on sample chapters and contributing a beautiful photograph to the book.

Thank you to Ruth O'Rourke, Barbara Zuniga, and Lucy Philpott at DK for your sensitive and expert handling of the manuscript and images, and for capturing the spirit of my work so well in the finished book. To my agent, Charlie Brotherstone, thank you for understanding and respecting my goals, and for your determination, patience, sensitivity, and boundless enthusiasm.

PUBLISHER'S ACKNOWLEDGMENTS

DK would like to thank Ridhima Sikka and Samrajkumar S for the picture research, Dawn Titmus for the proofread, Vanessa Bird for the index, and Adam Brackenbury and Tom Morse for the repro work on the images.

PICTURE CREDITS

The publisher would like to thank the following for their kind permission to reproduce their photographs:
(Key: a-above; b-below/bottom; c-centre; f-far; l-left; r-right; t-top)

123RF.com: Makkis 177tl; Alamy Stock Photo: Avalon.red / Photos Horticultural 179cla, Biosphoto / Alain Kubacsi 177tr, Chris Bosworth 175bc, Kevin Britland 177tc, Endless Travel 177cr, Florapix 173ca, 175ca, John Glover 181tl, Jani-Markus Häsä 181tr, Isabel 39br, Martin Hughes-Jones 181br, Kohl-Photo 179cl, Premium Stock Photography GmbH / Frank Teigler 173ca (6), RM Floral 177c (9), 181cl, Sally Smith 181cla, P Tomlins 175bl, Botany Vision 143br, Ray Wilson 177bc, Zoonar GmbH / Joerg Hemmer 165cb; Clive Nichols: 72–73; Depositphotos Inc: Belizar 179clb, Imagebroker 177c; Dorling Kindersley: Hampton Court Flower Show 2014 / Mark Winwood 161cr, Hester Robson 173c; Dreamstime.com: Anmbph 179bl, Leopoldo Barrios 179cra, John Biglin 173cra, Bykot30 173tr, CloudyTheater 180tl, Cristographic 175tc, Mark Van Dam 177br, DrewTraveler 176tl, Iuri Gagarin 178tl, Ruud Glasbergen 179crb, Nick Johnson 157tc, Anatolii Lyzun 179cb, Oleh Marchak 177cb, Mariuszks 173clb, Tom Meaker 175c, Nahhan 173cla, Simona Pavan 175cl, Ste208 181bc, Henk Wallays 175br, Christian Weiß 179c (9), Andrii Zhezhera 173tc; GAP Photos: 181bl, Thomas Alamy 181cr, Elke Borkowski 224, Jonathan Buckley 163bc, 173bc, Oscar DArcy 179bc, Garden World Images 179tl, Dianna Jazwinski 173cb, Terry Jennings 46b, Joanna Kossak 181cra, Caroline Mardon 181c, Jan Smith 159tc, Evgeniya Vlasova 163tc; Getty Images / iStock: Helena Bezold 179c, Yujie Chen 175tr, ChrisAt 172tl, DutchlightNetherlands 175tl, E+ / Tioloco 177ca, Emer1940 179tr, Kulbabka 179cr, Francesca Leslie 179ca, Cecile Meis 175clb, Mykhailo007 173bl, Pilesasmiles 174tl, Robitaille 175cra; Shutterstock.com: Penny Hicks 173tl, Matt Hirst 177clb, Maik Kellerhals 179tc, Lidia Kovacs 181tc, Joe Kuis 181crb, Tony Mills 177bl, Tatyana Mut 181clb, Uellue 177cla

All Other Images © Carol Bruce
Cover images: Carol Bruce

Editorial Director Ruth O'Rourke
Project Editor Lucy Philpott
Gardening Design Manager Barbara Zuniga
Senior Production Editor Tony Phipps
Senior Production Controller Stephanie McConnell
DTP and Design Coordinator Heather Blagden
Jacket and Sales Material Coordinator Serena Sclocco
Art Director Maxine Pedliham
Publishing Director Stephanie Jackson

Editorial Anna Kruger
Design Matt Cox at Newman+Eastwood Ltd
Illustration Stuart Jackson-Carter

First published in Great Britain in 2026 by
Dorling Kindersley Limited
20 Vauxhall Bridge Road,
London SW1V 2SA

The authorised representative in the EEA is
Dorling Kindersley Verlag GmbH. Arnulfstr. 124,
80636 Munich, Germany

Text copyright © Carol Bruce 2026
Carol Bruce has asserted her right to be identified
as the author of this work.
Copyright © 2026 Dorling Kindersley Limited
A Penguin Random House Company
10 9 8 7 6 5 4 3 2 1
001–358763–May/2026

All rights reserved.
No part of this publication may be reproduced, stored in or introduced into a retrieval system, or transmitted, in any form, or by any means (electronic, mechanical, photocopying, recording, or otherwise), without the prior written permission of the copyright owner.
DK values and supports copyright. Thank you for respecting intellectual property laws by not reproducing, scanning or distributing any part of this publication by any means without permission. By purchasing an authorised edition, you are supporting writers and artists and enabling DK to continue to publish books that inform and inspire readers.
No part of this publication may be used or reproduced in any manner for the purpose of training artificial intelligence technologies or systems. In accordance with Article 4(3) of the DSM Directive 2019/790, DK expressly reserves this work from the text and data mining exception.

A CIP catalogue record for this book
is available from the British Library.
ISBN: 978-0-2418-0671-5

Printed and bound in China

www.dk.com

This book was made with Forest Stewardship Council™ certified paper – one small step in DK's commitment to a sustainable future. Learn more at www.dk.com/uk/information/sustainability

ABOUT THE AUTHOR

Born in suburban South East England in 1969, Carol Bruce grew up with an unshakeable desire to live in the woods, and an innate drive to examine the forces that stand between us and our connection to nature. After studying economics at the University of Cambridge, she began methodically exploring new ways of relating to the natural world that can bring sustainability and artistry onto the same page, resulting in the creation of a garden and a philosophy that are a fusion of both. She opens her award-winning garden at Old Bladbean Stud for charity through the National Garden Scheme, and shares the garden's progress through the seasons via Facebook. Carol makes nature-inspired jewellery for a living, which is marketed through her Etsy shop Reweaving the Rainbow, and she spends all her spare time peacefully walking in the woods.

www.oldbladbeanstud.co.uk
www.reweavingtherainbow.etsy.com
Facebook: Old Bladbean Stud Gardens